THE
LIBERATION
OF
PARIS

"I read Jean Edward Smith's *The Liberation of Paris* with tears in my eyes and huge admiration. It is still one of the most moving moments in the history of the Second World War—I remember my mother opening a bottle of champagne and singing 'La Marseillaise' when we heard the news—and Jean portrays not only the drama and suspense of the event, but the character of the people who were involved, in a very objective way, giving full weight to the profound importance of General de Gaulle, and to the crucial role of General Eisenhower, for which he has never received sufficient credit. This is great history."
—Michael Korda, author of *Ike: An American Hero*

"Jean Edward Smith is a marvelous historian, and in his latest work he does not disappoint. *The Liberation of Paris* is a scintillating and fascinating book. How was one of the great cities of the world saved? It's a rousing tale. Bravo!"
—Jay Winik, author of *1944* and *April 1865*

"*The Liberation of Paris* in August 1944 has to be one of history's happiest moments. . . . It is still a great story in Jean Edward Smith's trim but engaging account of driving darkness from the City of Light."
—Evan Thomas, *Air Mail*

"*The Liberation of Paris* is a remarkable story that shows how three men from warring sides of an epic struggle saved Paris. Smith's book is a must-read that brims with heroism, intrigue, chaos, and danger."

—Susan Eisenhower

"Smith does an exemplary job of highlighting how the German military commander of Paris, General der Infanterie Dietrich von Choltitz, was determined to save Paris from the moment he was appointed its commander by Adolf Hitler. . . . *The Liberation of Paris* is a quick read and builds suspense as it investigates key players and decisions and provides context to one of the great 'unknown' stories of World War II."

—Col. Kevin W. Farrell, (U.S.A.– Ret.), *ARMY* magazine

"An outstanding concise history of one of the most dramatic moments of WWII: the liberation of the City of Light in August 1944. . . . Smith is an outstanding historian and tells a dramatic story well. This is a solid contribution to the history of WWII that both the general reader and the expert will find enjoyable and informative."

—*Publishers Weekly*

"Smith, a WWII expert, examines the fascinating circumstances surrounding the liberation of Paris. . . . A fascinating chapter in the larger of story of the Allied victory in Europe."

—*Booklist*

"Eminent historian Smith has such a breadth of knowledge of this era in history that he is able to offer a distillation of swift-moving events surrounding the 1944 liberation of Paris in a marvelously readable fashion. . . . A succinctly instructive historical narrative by a top-notch historian and author."

—*Kirkus Reviews*

ALSO BY JEAN EDWARD SMITH

Bush

Eisenhower in War and Peace

FDR

Grant

John Marshall: Definer of a Nation

George Bush's War

Lucius D. Clay: An American Life

The Conduct of American Foreign Policy Debated
(ed., with Herbert M. Levine)

The Constitution and American Foreign Policy

Civil Liberties and Civil Rights Debated
(ed., with Herbert M. Levine)

The Papers of General Lucius D. Clay (ed.)

Germany Beyond the Wall

Der Weg ins Dilemma

The Defense of Berlin

THE

LIBERATION

OF

PARIS

How Eisenhower, de Gaulle,
and von Choltitz Saved
the City of Light

JEAN EDWARD SMITH

Simon & Schuster Paperbacks

NEW YORK · LONDON · TORONTO · SYDNEY · NEW DELHI

Simon & Schuster Paperbacks
An Imprint of Simon & Schuster, Inc.
1230 Avenue of the Americas
New York, NY 10020

First Simon & Schuster paperback edition July 2020

SIMON & SCHUSTER PAPERBACKS and colophon are registered trademarks of Simon & Schuster, Inc.

For information about special discounts for bulk purchases, please contact Simon & Schuster Special Sales at 1-866-506-1949 or business@simonandschuster.com.

The Simon & Schuster Speakers Bureau can bring authors to your live event. For more information or to book an event, contact the Simon & Schuster Speakers Bureau at 1-866-248-3049 or visit our website at www.simonspeakers.com.

Manufactured in the United States of America

1   3   5   7   9   10   8   6   4   2

The Library of Congress has cataloged the hardcover edition as follows:

Names: Smith, Jean Edward, author.
Title: The liberation of Paris : how Eisenhower, De Gaulle, and Von Choltitz saved the City of Light / Jean Edward Smith.
Description: First Simon & Schuster hardcover edition. | New York : Simon & Schuster, 2019. | "Simon & Schuster nonfiction original hardcover." | Includes bibliographical references and index.
Identifiers: LCCN 2018036260| ISBN 9781501164927 | ISBN 1501164929 | ISBN 9781501164941 (ebook)
Subjects: LCSH: Paris (France)—History—1940-1944. | France—History—German occupation, 1940-1945. | World War, 1939-1945—France—Paris.
Classification: LCC D762.P3 S65 2019 | DDC 940.54/214361--dc23
LC record available at https://lccn.loc.gov/2018036260

ISBN 978-1-5011-6492-7
ISBN 978-1-5011-6493-4 (pbk)
ISBN 978-1-5011-6494-1 (ebook)

For Christine

Contents

THE
LIBERATION
OF
PARIS

— I —

Paris Occupied

"Paris has always fascinated me. . . . I could have marched at the head of my troops under the Arc de Triomphe . . . but I did not want, under any pretext, to inflict this humiliation on the French people after their defeat. I want no obstacle to this Franco-German entente, which will happen, I am sure."

—ADOLF HITLER, PARIS, JUNE 28, 1940

German troops entered Paris in the early morning hours of June 14, 1940. There was no fighting, and no shots were exchanged. French general Maxime Weygand, the army's commander in chief, had declared Paris an open city, and it was not defended. On June 10, the French government had fled first to Tours, then to Bordeaux, and the army withdrew shortly afterward. Unlike World War I, in which the French army defended the approaches to Paris successfully in 1914 and again in 1918, this time the army withdrew without a fight. The French leadership recognized that the war was lost, and chose not to defend the capital city. Paris, with a population of four million and incomparable art treasures and historic monuments, became German territory overnight. General Fedor von Bock, commanding German Army Group B, held a quick review of his troops at the Place de la Concorde early on the morning of June 14, and then had breakfast at the Ritz.

1

General von Bock saluting his troops entering Paris, June 14, 1940

The beginnings of World War II, and the history of France preceding it, must be understood to appreciate the significance of the German occupation of Paris. After German forces invaded Poland on September 1, 1939, Britain and France, honoring their diplomatic obligations, declared war on Germany. That decision was not popular in France. There were no supportive demonstrations in Paris or other French cities when war came, no ringing declarations of the righteousness of the war or the evils of Hitler's regime. France mobilized an army of 2.6 million men. But they took up defensive positions, half on the Maginot Line, the other half on the Belgian border, ready to meet another German Schlieffen Plan that would outflank the French army by moving through Belgium, as in 1914. Many Frenchmen doubted the wisdom of the government's going to war. The French right admired Hitler and Nazi Germany. For them, the war was indefensible. The left, though they despised Nazi totalitarianism, did not want war with any country, because of a devotion to pacifism and a conviction, taught in public schools since 1919, that war was an evil to be avoided at all costs. France's enormous losses in World War I contributed to that feeling.

After the surprise signing of the Hitler-Stalin nonaggression pact on August 23, 1939, the Soviet Union joined Germany and invaded Poland on September 17, 1939. By September 29 that war was over. Germany and the Soviet Union divided Poland—the fourth time Poland had been dismembered—and Britain and France had done nothing to prevent it. Why the French did not attack Germany while the German army was deployed in Poland remains a mystery. As Field Marshal Wilhelm Keitel, the chief of the German high command, said later, "We soldiers had always expected an attack by France during the Polish campaign and were very much surprised when nothing happened. . . . A French attack would have encountered only a German military screen, not a real defense." [1]

The decision of Stalin to join with Hitler complicated political alignments within France. The French Communist Party (PCF), under orders from Moscow, endorsed the partition of Poland and denounced France's decision to join with Great Britain in an imperialist war against Germany. "The people of France have been assigned the mission of executing the orders of the bankers of London," said the PCF in October. [2]

After the fall of Poland, France still did not attack Germany. Russia invaded Finland on November 30, but France was not involved. For the next five months the French and German armies faced each other without a shot being fired. The French called it *drôle de guerre.* The Germans called it *Sitzkrieg.* During that period French military morale suffered badly. It was largely a draftee army; pay was minimal, and with no fighting it seemed a waste of time. At the governmental level, Édouard Daladier, who had succeeded Léon Blum as prime minister in April 1938, resigned on March 20, 1940, and was succeeded by Paul Reynaud.

The situation changed abruptly on April 9, 1940, when Germany invaded Denmark and Norway. The Danish invasion took only four hours, and by noon on the 9th the Germans were in total control. No shots had been fired. In Norway, the exercise took longer, but the outcome was never in doubt. All of Norway's ports as well as the capital of Oslo were captured by the Germans on the first day. The British fleet intervened briefly; a number of German vessels were sunk, and the port of Narvik was retaken. But resistance was marginalized, and Norway, like Denmark, became occupied.

The taking of Denmark and Norway was a prelude to what was about to happen. In Paris, Prime Minister Reynaud was distraught that his military leadership had not been able to assist Norway, and he began to doubt the competence of General Maurice Gamelin, the commander in chief of the army who had succeeded Maxime Weygand in 1935. But before he could replace Gamelin, the Germans invaded. Rather than an attack on the Maginot Line, or the mounting of another Schlieffen Plan through Belgium, the principal attack came in the Ardennes, directly between the two French forces. In 1934, Marshal Pétain, the hero of Verdun, in testimony before the French chamber of deputies, had said, "The Ardennes are impregnable. . . . As the front will have no depth, the enemy will not be able to engage in action there. And if he does, he will be picked up as he emerges from the forests. So this sector is not dangerous."[3] The French had planned accordingly.

The Germans decided exactly the opposite. Rather than attack the French in their dug-in positions, they would crash through the Ardennes (Figure 1). In what was known as the Manstein Plan, for Erich von Manstein, the chief of staff to General Gerd

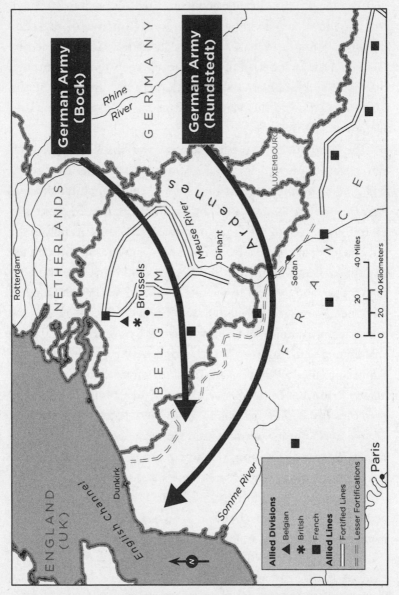

Figure 1: The Fall of France, May 1940

von Rundstedt, the Germans concentrated on breaking through the Ardennes and dividing French forces in two. In the early morning hours of May 10, Rundstedt's Army Group A, led by General Heinz Guderian's XIX armored corps, moved through the forest and mountains of the Ardennes with lightning speed. They pressed on to the Meuse River, and by May 15 had taken Dinant and Sedan.*

The Germans proved adept at tank warfare. When the invasion began on May 10, they had 2,580 tanks available. The French had 2,800, and most experts considered the French tanks superior. But the French tanks were distributed across the front into each division. All of the German tanks were concentrated in the ten Panzer divisions that led Rundstedt's army group through the Ardennes. It was no match. The French could not stop the German armor, and by May 20 the Germans had reached the English Channel. France was divided in two. Gamelin was relieved as the army's commander in chief and replaced by Weygand, and Marshal Pétain, who had been France's ambassador to Spain, became deputy premier, all to no avail. Belgium surrendered on May 28, and by June 4, the British Expeditionary Force, more than 300,000 men plus 130,000 French soldiers, were evacuated from Dunkirk. France north of the Somme was in German hands. No more than half of Weygand's divisions remained. On June 10, Mussolini entered the war, and French forces were spread further.

Resistance proved futile. On June 12 Weygand ordered a general retreat; Paris was declared an open city, and the German army moved south quickly. On June 16, General Rommel's armored

---

* According to General Günther Blumentritt, chief of operations for Army Group A, the move through the Ardennes "was not really an operation but an approach march. . . . We met only slight resistance in Belgian Luxembourg. . . . It was weak opposition and easily brushed aside." B. H. Liddell Hart, *The German Generals Talk* (New York: William Morrow, 1948), 106.

division moved 240 kilometers through Brittany without firing a shot. Reynaud stepped down as prime minister on June 16 and was succeeded by Marshal Pétain, who immediately sought an armistice. On June 22, six weeks after the invasion began, the war was over. The armistice was signed in the same railroad car in the same forest clearing near Compiègne where the World War I armistice had been signed.

Under the armistice, which was intended to be a temporary agreement pending a formal peace treaty, Germany occupied much of northern France, the entire west coast, and Paris. Alsace

Figure 2: Occupied France

and Lorraine were detached and became provinces in the Third Reich, and Italy was later awarded a small occupation zone in the Alps. (See Figure 2.) The purpose of the occupation was to facilitate Germany's invasion of Great Britain, which was expected shortly. The costs of the occupation were to be paid by the French. Most important, the French government remained sovereign. It could choose where it wanted to be located, including Paris, but the occupied zone must conform to German authority.* The French army was demobilized and disarmed, and all of its equipment turned over to the Germans. Captured French soldiers remained in German custody, and, like Germany after the Versailles treaty, France was permitted an army of 100,000 men, but without heavy weapons.

The French navy was treated somewhat better. It was required to collect in French ports, but "the German government solemnly declares to the French government that it does not intend to use the French war fleet which is in harbors under German control for its purposes in war."[4] The armistice was signed for France by General Charles Léon Huntziger, who later commanded the hundred thousand men. Said Huntziger, "France has the right to expect in the future negotiations that Germany will show a spirit which will permit the two great neighboring countries to live and work in peace."[5]

The armistice went into effect on June 25. Marshal Pétain spoke to the nation that day. Instead of acknowledging that France's de-

---

* According to Article III, "The French Government is permitted to select the seat of its government in unoccupied territory, or, if it wishes, in Paris. In this case, the German government guarantees the French Government and its central authorities every necessary alleviation so that they will be in a position to conduct the administration of unoccupied territories from Paris." Armistice Agreement, June 22, 1940, U.S. Department of State, *Documents on German Foreign Policy, 1918–1945* (Washington, DC: Government Printing Office, 1956), 671–676.

feat was a result of military ineptitude, he suggested that French attitudes dominant in the Third Republic had brought about its downfall. "Our defeat came because of our slackness. The seeking of pleasures destroyed what the spirit of sacrifice had built up. I call upon you first of all for intellectual and moral redress. . . . A New Order begins."[6]

The days of the Third Republic were numbered. Like many Frenchmen at the time, Pétain blamed the secular democracy of the Third Republic for France's defeat. Or as the Catholic Church put it, France had received "divine retribution" for its godless ways. On July 3, Britain helped fuel the fire when under Churchill's orders it destroyed much of the French fleet at the Algerian port of Mers-el-Kébir, killing 1,267 French sailors. The tension

Pétain, May 1940

with Great Britain grew enormously, and Pétain broke off diplomatic relations.

When the Chamber of Deputies and the Senate met in the new capital at Vichy on July 9, the French representatives voted 624 to 4 that the constitution should be revised. As the historian Robert Paxton has noted, "The Assembly's stand of July 9, 1940, was no revolution from above. It reflected almost unanimous French public opinion."[7] The following day, by a vote of 569 to 80, the Assembly installed Pétain with full power to lead the new French State. Pierre Laval became Pétain's deputy, and the motto of the Third Republic, "*Liberté, égalité, fraternité,*" was replaced with "*Travail, famille, patrie*"—"Work, family, fatherland." The French had voluntarily turned against the secular democracy of the Third Republic. Masculine dominance, anti-Semitism, and the leadership of the Roman Catholic Church became the order of the day. These were French decisions and not of German imposition.

President Roosevelt and the U.S. State Department quickly recognized the Pétain government. The American embassy was moved from Paris to Vichy, and FDR appointed Admiral William Leahy, the former chief of naval operations, to be ambassador. Leahy was an old friend of the president going back to the days when Roosevelt was assistant secretary of the navy in the Woodrow Wilson administration, and FDR believed that he and Pétain would hit it off together.

At the time, most French people believed that Great Britain would soon be defeated. The German army was also on its best behavior. "Keep Paris Paris" was the order of the day. Tourism was encouraged, and the city was soon filled with busloads of uniformed German troops. There was no resistance. It was difficult for the French to believe that the war was not over. Even the underground Communist newspaper *L'Humanité* urged a peace of reconciliation between French and German workers. Germans felt likewise. "Paris remains one of the jewels of Europe," Hitler told his generals, and that attitude dominated the early occupation.[8] As the Paris magazine *L'Illustration* wrote in the fall of 1940:

> What struck us at the sight of the military men moving among us was their obvious youth. Under the *feldgrau* uniform, we could not distinguish social class or profession. But we could sense there were many intellectuals among the young people, university students who would take up their interrupted studies and who would profit from their visit to learn about French culture. . . . This occasion would help

Hitler in Paris, 1940

them, to their benefit, to see the real face of France, to be able to get to know its citizens, and to familiarize themselves with our customs and our spirit.[9]

Given the subsequent resistance in Paris, it is difficult to remember that in 1940 not only did peace prevail, but almost everyone in France assumed that Germany would soon be the victor over Great Britain. Paris had opened its gates to the German army, and the army reciprocated. Paris became "Germanized" overnight. The combination of the effortless control and correct behavior exercised by the German army (unlike its later behavior in Eastern Europe) and the armistice that had preserved a portion of French honor made the occupation of Paris embarrassingly simple. As one scholar of the period has written, "Paris had become a suburb of Berlin."[10]

To head the occupation, Hitler named sixty-two-year-old General Otto von Stülpnagel, who was then commanding German troops in Austria. Stülpnagel established the German headquarters in the Hotel Majestic, and did his best to ensure friendly relations. "If you want a cow to give milk, it must be fed," he said in September 1940.[11] He emphasized the need to cooperate with French industry, deplored the confiscation of Jewish art collections, and resisted orders from Berlin to execute large numbers of hostages. In February 1942, when ordered by Field Marshal Keitel to execute imprisoned Communists and Jews, he submitted a bitter letter of resignation and retired from active duty.

He was succeeded by his cousin, General Karl Heinrich von Stülpnagel, who had been a combat general on the Russian front and was familiar with execution orders. At the same time, he despised Hitler and the Nazis, and would become a leading member of the military's July 20, 1944, plot to assassinate the Führer. That afternoon, when told that Colonel Claus von Stauffenberg's bomb had exploded in the room where Hitler was holding a meeting, he assumed the Führer was dead and ordered the arrest of all Gestapo and SS officers in Paris. The arrests took place, but that evening it became clear that Hitler had survived. The arrested men were released and Stülpnagel was recalled to Berlin. Tried for treason by the People's Court in Berlin on August 30, he was convicted and hanged that same day at Plötzensee Prison in Berlin. Both Stülpnagels were enthralled by Paris, and had done their best to preserve it unscathed.

The chief German diplomat in Paris was Otto Abetz, who was appointed ambassador to Vichy by Hitler but who chose to reside in Paris. Abetz was thirty-seven at the time, a close friend of Foreign Minister Joachim von Ribbentrop, and like the Stülpnagels, he was eager to keep Franco-German relations cordial. An art teacher before the war, he had helped found the Stolberg Circle, later known as the Franco-German Committee (*Comité France-Allemagne*), which promoted cultural exchanges. He had been married to a French woman since 1932, admired French culture, and immediately established as an appendix to the embassy a German Institute where Parisians could study German culture and learn the language. Throughout the occupation, the German army and the diplomatic corps did their best to observe the rules of international behavior. Whatever cruelty happened in Paris was the work of the Gestapo and SS, as well as the Vichy regime. Also like the Stülpnagels, Abetz often fought with the Gestapo and the SS. He remained in Paris until the liberation.

Life in Paris returned to normal almost immediately after the occupation began. Movie houses started showing films the following week. On July 31, barely six weeks since German troops entered the city, Sacha Guitry reopened the Théâtre de la Madeleine with his play *Pasteur*. The play ended with the audience rising to sing *La Marseillaise*, led by the German administrative head of Paris, General Harald Turner. The Paris Opera resumed on August 24 with Berlioz's *La Damnation de Faust*, followed by Massenet's *Thaïs* and Beethoven's *Fidelio*. The Comédie-Française started performances on September 7 with a program designed by Vichy proclaiming hope for France because it was amending its errors of the past. On September 29, Field Marshal von Rundstedt attended the reopening of the Louvre.* At the Orangerie, on the Place de la Concorde, where Monet's *Nymphéas* paintings hung, a retrospective of Monet and Rodin brought huge crowds.[12]

Perhaps the only downside in Paris was the treatment of Jews and Freemasons on orders that came directly from the Vichy government. Freemasons, whom most French clerics considered henchmen of the devil, but who were in many respects the backbone of the Third Republic, were hit on August 13, 1940, when Vichy dismantled their lodges and banned all members from public functions. Then, on October 3, Vichy promulgated a Statute on Jews—the first anti-Semitic measure of the Pétain regime. Under the act, Jews were excluded from the civil service, the judiciary, the armed forces, the press, and the teaching profession. Anti-Semitism was not new to France, but it became one of the hallmarks of the Vichy regime. The Statute on Jews illustrated the Vichy government's willingness to act on its own authority without German pressure and was an ominous sign for the future.[13]

At the time, Charles de Gaulle was unknown by most Parisians. A colonel on active duty when the war began, he did well in combat, was promoted to brigadier general, and when Reynaud became prime minister was made undersecretary of the Ministry of National Defense. De Gaulle had written extensively on armored

---

* On July 19, 1940, Army Group commanders Rundstedt, Bock, and Leeb were promoted by Hitler to the rank of field marshal. Wilhelm von Leeb had commanded Army Group C during the invasion.

warfare, had become a friend of Reynaud during the prewar period, and his appointment gave Reynaud a vantage point from which to influence the military. Neither Pétain nor Weygand was pleased with the appointment. "He's an infant," Weygand told Reynaud. "He is more a journalist than an officer." Pétain's judgment was harsher. "He's an arrogant man, an ingrate, and surly," said the marshal. "He has few friends in the Army . . . for he gives the impression he is looking down on everybody."[14] When defeat came, de Gaulle flew to London with British general Edward Spears, met with Churchill, and on June 18 delivered a stirring address over BBC to the French population. "Whatever happens, the flame of French resistance must not and shall not die."[15] Very few in France heard de Gaulle speak. The fact that he was speaking from London

Pétain and Hitler

did not help. The BBC did not record it, and de Gaulle remained in the wilderness as far as the citizens of Paris were concerned.

French cooperation with Germany continued. In late October first Laval, then Pétain, met with Hitler at Montoire in southern France as the Führer went to visit Generalissimo Francisco Franco in Spain. Speaking afterward at the Matignon Palace in Paris, under a French flag, Laval said, "In all domains, and especially in the economic and colonial spheres, we have discussed and we will continue to examine in what practical form our collaboration can serve the interests of France, Germany, and Europe."

Pétain famously said, "I enter into the way of collaboration. In the near future, the weight of suffering of our country could be lightened, the fate of our prisoners ameliorated, occupation costs reduced, the demarcation line made more flexible, and the administration and supply of our territory easier."[16]

Parisians adjusted surprisingly well to the occupation. Many became active collaborators. The Germans were in charge, and everyday Parisians made the best of it. As the writer Alan Riding has pointed out, "For some cabaret managers, it was as if *la belle époque* were back."[17] To the surprise of many, Hitler announced that the ashes of Napoléon I's son, the Duc de Reichstadt, would be returned from Vienna and buried at Les Invalides on December 15, 1940, the hundredth anniversary of Napoléon's burial there.

Change came slowly. Rationing was introduced in Paris in the autumn of 1940, and gasoline was in short supply. By the spring of 1941 it looked as if the war was going to last considerably longer than most Parisians had anticipated. Under Churchill's leadership the British were still fighting. Hitler had canceled the invasion of Great Britain, and the lengthy German air attacks on that country had proved fruitless. Germany had not gained air superiority. Then on June 22, 1941, the situation changed dramatically. Without prior warning, the German army invaded the Soviet Union.

In Paris, French Communists changed sides overnight, becoming enemies of the occupation. In many respects, the resistance to Hitler by a significant number of Parisians dates to this event.

Parisians became even more uncomfortable in December 1941, when the Japanese attacked Pearl Harbor. Germany and Italy declared war on the United States immediately afterward, and the United States responded by declaring war on December 11. In November 1942, American troops landed in the French colonies of Morocco and Algeria in North Africa. The German government responded by occupying all of France. The situation changed further on January 30, 1943, when the German Sixth Army under Field Marshal Friedrich von Paulus surrendered at Stalingrad. The Germans lost more than 200,000 men. For Parisians it looked as though the tide had turned. That seemed to be confirmed, on May 13, 1943, when Anglo-American forces accepted the German surrender in North Africa, where Germany lost another 290,000 men. The Wehrmacht now looked vulnerable.

When Hitler moved into Vichy territory in December 1942 following the Allied invasion of North Africa, he chose to retain the Pétain regime. "French sovereignty will be maintained," said Hitler, "but only in so far as it serves our interests."[18] By continuing to maintain the French State, Germany would be able to obtain whatever it wanted, and use the state apparatus as it wished. Hitler also told Pétain that he wanted Laval to remain as the head of government.[19] Under Hitler's orders the 100,000-man French army was disarmed and demobilized. Laval responded in January 1943 by establishing the French Militia (*la Milice*), a police force of volunteers whose task it would be to maintain order.

In Paris life went on, but the occupation was now becoming onerous. The most despicable aspect of it was the treatment of the Jews, which was getting worse. When the war began in 1939, there were about 300,000 Jews living in France, with roughly 60 percent in Paris. Since 1791, when the National Assembly had granted Jews full civil rights, Paris had been a "new Jerusalem," and many European Jews sought refuge there. In 1936, France chose a Jew, Léon Blum, to be prime minister, the first European state ever to do so. But on May 14, 1941, the Paris police conducted their first roundup of Jews, sending almost four thousand to internment camps.[20] Roundups continued throughout 1941 and 1942, and by the end of 1942, almost forty thousand Jews had been deported.

The Germans joined the persecution, commanded by SS *Standartenführer* Helmut Knochen, and on May 29, 1942, issued an order requiring Jewish citizens above the age of six to wear a yellow Star of David. A few weeks later Jews were excluded from public places (cafés, theaters, libraries, swimming pools, and parks) and prohibited from shopping until the afternoon, when there was hardly anything left in the food stores. The *standartenführer* SS and Gestapo looted Jewish property, taking artwork and furnishings from apartments formerly occupied by Parisian Jews. When the occupation ended, eighty thousand Jews had been sent to concentration camps, and of those twenty-four thousand were of French nationality, the other fifty-six thousand being more recent arrivals. Only 3 percent returned alive. Bad as that may seem, it was considerably better than what happened in Belgium and Holland. And it was better because of the help provided by many French, to shield their Jewish neighbors.[21]

Daily life in Paris became more difficult for everyone, unless you had money or were a collaborationist. The Germans had turned Paris into a place of recreation for soldiers on leave. German officers felt at home in the Tour d'Argent and other gastronomic temples, all of which provided special menus in German. French companions were plentiful, but they were mostly collaborationists, cultural icons, or the upper crust of French society. After the war, and looking back at the occupation, Jean-Paul Sartre wrote, "I wonder if I shall be understood if I say that it [the occupation] was both intolerable and at the same time we put up with it very well."[22]

Cultural life in Paris continued undisturbed. Classical German music led the way. Parisians had always been fond of German music, and compositions by Bach, Handel, Mozart, Beethoven, and Wagner continued to be constantly performed, often by German orchestras, including the Berlin Philharmonic. The young conductor Herbert von Karajan, of the Berlin *Staatsoper* (State Opera), became a favorite of Parisians and led the *Staatsoper* in numerous concerts in Paris.[23]

French filmmaking also prospered. Between June 1940 and the liberation in August 1944, the film industry produced a record 220 films. German censorship, aside from banning British and American films, was minimal, and the Germans encouraged French filmmakers to produce quality entertainment. By 1943, movie attendance in Paris was 40 percent higher than in 1938— the last year before the war—and Parisians flocked to the cinema to escape the drudgery of everyday life.[24]

For French writers, the occupation also provided a unique opportunity. Many became ardent collaborationists; others went underground. The written word, unlike the theater or music, is in black-and-white, and the author can be judged accordingly. It would be fair to say that for the first two years of the occupation, French writers generally cooperated with the occupiers. But when it became clear that the Germans were losing, writers became more critical. German policy was set by Goebbels and his propaganda ministry, and most of the effort was directed at silencing Jewish writers or anti-German books.

Social relations between Germans and Parisians were encouraged. German soldiers and French women hit it off amazingly well. By mid-1943, more than eighty thousand French women claimed benefits for their offspring from the German authorities. Those women who had affairs with Germans spanned the social ladder, and many Parisians of high social standing took up with German suitors. The famous actress Arletty and the designer Coco Chanel lived with German officers at the Ritz. "My heart is French but my ass is international," said Arletty after the war.[25]

But the tide was turning in 1943. American and British troops captured Sicily in July, and in the east the Soviet army was advancing. In Paris, sympathy for the occupation was diminishing rapidly. And the support for Pétain and the Vichy regime was eroding even faster. For Parisians, the high points of the occupation were the years 1940 and 1941, when German victory in Europe seemed inevitable. But as the military situation changed, so too did French attitudes toward the occupation.

Unlike London or Berlin, Paris had not been bombed, and the city remained intact. That was a blessing, but the Germans were exploiting the French economy, and the costs were hitting home. French agricultural products had been taken increasingly to feed Germany, and the German war machine was fueled by French industry. By 1943, well over half of French agricultural production was going to German cities. This created serious shortages in Paris, where almost all food was rationed. In addition, almost a million young Frenchmen had been sent to Germany to work in industry, and the war prisoners still held by the Germans added to the total.

The occupation had come full circle. What began in 1940 as an acceptance and even celebration of German victory had by the beginning of 1944 become a desperate undertaking. Collaborationists were beginning to look for cover, and the Resistance, which was negligible in 1940, was becoming a factor to be reckoned with. As Yves Bouthillier, who served as Pétain's finance minister, wrote, "Public opinion, initially so favorable, even enthusiastic, became doubtful, suspicious, distrustful, and eventually, little by little, hostile. The divorce began slowly around the middle of 1941, at first it was imperceptible, a hair-line crack, but from 1942 onwards it became even wider and more obvious."[26] When 1944 began, most Parisians realized that Germany was losing the war, and that set off a tide of reaction.

— II —

De Gaulle and the Resistance

"Paris must be liberated by French troops."

—DE GAULLE TO EISENHOWER, DECEMBER 30, 1943

An even more dramatic change in Paris by 1944 reflected the growing enthusiasm for the leadership of Charles de Gaulle. At the beginning of the German blitzkrieg on May 10, 1940, de Gaulle was a colonel commanding a tank regiment in Alsace. Less than two weeks later he was promoted to brigadier general on the battlefield, and on June 6 was appointed by Prime Minister Paul Reynaud to be undersecretary of state for national defense in the French cabinet. He and Reynaud were old acquaintances, and the prime minister believed de Gaulle would provide valuable support in the cabinet. Ten days later, as military defeat became evident, de Gaulle was instructed by Reynaud to go to London and request Churchill's assistance to help move the French government to North Africa, from which the war could continue.

De Gaulle arrived in London on the morning of Sunday, June 16. Meeting with French ambassador Charles Corbin and Jean Monnet, a prominent French businessman, before seeing Churchill, he was told of a plan they had been working on with the British Foreign Office to unite France and Great Britain into one country—a "Declaration of Union." There would be a common constitution, one government, common citizenship, and a complete linking of their respective destinies. Churchill was aware of the plan, but he had not yet discussed it with the British cabinet. Would de Gaulle press him to do so? they asked.

De Gaulle was enthusiastic about the plan. He recognized that it could not be brought into effect overnight, but thought it would give Reynaud valuable support to continue the war. He agreed to raise the matter with Churchill when they met for lunch later that day. When de Gaulle restated the proposal, Churchill said that Lord Halifax, the British foreign minister, had told him of the plan. "But it is an enormous mouthful."[1] De Gaulle agreed, but said to announce it would greatly benefit the Reynaud government and help keep France in the war. Churchill understood and said he would present it to his cabinet that afternoon. De Gaulle accompanied him to 10 Downing Street, where he waited in an office adjoining the Cabinet Room.

While the cabinet meeting was going on, de Gaulle phoned Reynaud to tell him what was happening. Reynaud said he thought it was "the only possible solution for the future, but it must be done very quickly, above all quickly."[2] The British cabinet meeting lasted almost two hours, during which various ministers came out to ask de Gaulle to clarify something. Then a beaming Churchill led the cabinet into the room where de Gaulle was waiting. "We are agreed," said the prime minister. De Gaulle immediately called Reynaud with the news. Churchill then took the phone and told Reynaud, "De Gaulle is right. . . . You must hold out. . . . We will see you tomorrow! At Concarneau."[3] Reynaud was overwhelmed by the British offer and said he would present it to his cabinet, which was to meet shortly.

It was at that meeting of the French cabinet late on June 16 that Reynaud lost his support. When he presented the proposal for an Anglo-French Union, the cabinet response was overwhelmingly negative. "A marriage with a corpse," said Marshal Pétain. "Better to be a Nazi province," said another. "At least we know what that means."[4] Only Georges Mandel, the minister of the interior, spoke in favor. Instead of supporting Reynaud's proposal for union with Britain, the cabinet went on to endorse a suggestion made by Camille Chautemps, a former prime minister, that Hitler should be asked for surrender terms and that they should be considered. At that point Reynaud adjourned the meeting, and then submitted his resignation to President Albert Lebrun.

The Reynaud government was finished. De Gaulle, en route back from London in a plane provided by Churchill, was told when he landed of Reynaud's defeat. The news that President Lebrun had appointed Pétain to be prime minister came shortly afterward. De Gaulle was stunned. He was no longer in the government, and Pétain as prime minister meant that French surrender was imminent.

De Gaulle went to see Reynaud immediately. "I found him with no illusions about what the consequences would be of the Marshal's taking power," said de Gaulle.[5] Reynaud said he intended to remain in France, although no longer in office. De Gaulle said he would return to England the next morning and continue the fight. "I didn't want to stay in Bordeaux with Pétain and Weygand."[6] Reynaud encouraged de Gaulle and gave him a hundred thousand francs from secret funds to which he still had access. De Gaulle then asked Reynaud's aide to have diplomatic passports sent to his wife and children so they could join him. Jean Laurent, who was on Reynaud's staff, gave de Gaulle the keys to an apartment he had in London and told him he could stay there as long as he wished. Shortly after nine the next morning, de Gaulle took off for England on the same plane that had brought him to France the night before. He had no government position and no idea of what might lie ahead, but he did not believe the war was over.

"I was starting from scratch," said de Gaulle. "But this very destitution showed me my line of conduct. It was by adopting without compromise the cause of national recovery that I could acquire authority. . . . It was by acting as the inflexible champion of the nation and of the state that it would be possible for me to gather the consent, even the enthusiasm, of the French and to win from foreigners respect and consideration. . . . In short, limited and alone though I was, and precisely because I was so, I had to climb to the heights and then never to come down."[7]

De Gaulle began his ascent immediately. His speech to the French nation over BBC the next evening is generally regarded as one of his greatest. "This war is not over as a result of the Battle of France," he said. "This war is a worldwide war. . . . I, General de Gaulle, currently in London, invite the officers and the French soldiers who are located in British territory or who might end up

De Gaulle in London, June 1940

here . . . to put themselves in contact with me. . . . The flame of French resistance must not and shall not die."[8]

The following day de Gaulle spoke again. "Soldiers of France, wherever you are, rise up."[9] His speech was so strong that the British Foreign Office intervened. The Pétain government had not yet signed the armistice, and the British did not want to provoke them needlessly. Not until the armistice was concluded and its terms revealed was de Gaulle given the go-ahead. It was during this period that both de Gaulle and Churchill hoped to recruit leading French personalities to join the resistance cause, but none came forward. Even those in London who wanted to go on fighting were not interested in attaching themselves to a crusade led by an obscure general. Finally, on June 27, Churchill bit the bullet. "You are alone," he told de Gaulle. "I shall recognize you alone."[10] The following day, official recognition followed. "His Majesty's government recognizes General de Gaulle as the leader of all Free Frenchmen, wherever they may be, who rally to him in support of the Allied cause."[11]

Six weeks later, on August 7, de Gaulle and Churchill signed a formal agreement in which the British agreed to supply and equip the Free French, and in return de Gaulle would follow the general orders of the British High Command, while retaining "supreme command" of his forces. The agreement "had a considerable importance for Free France," said de Gaulle, "not only because it got us out of immediate material difficulties, but also because the British authorities . . . no longer hesitated to make things easier for us."[12]

At the same time as de Gaulle was being formally recognized by His Majesty's government as the supreme commander of the Free French, he was being tried for treason in absentia by court-martial in Vichy. The charges were brought at the insistence of General Weygand, who believed de Gaulle was a traitor. The

Churchill and de Gaulle, 1940

trial was held in secret, and de Gaulle was found guilty on five of six counts. He was stripped of rank in the French army and sentenced to death, and his property was confiscated. De Gaulle does not refer to the trial in his memoirs, and for practical purposes the conviction was meaningless.

The British increased their support for de Gaulle quickly. Free French headquarters moved to spacious accommodations on Carlton Gardens overlooking St. James's Park—the former home of Prime Minister Lord Palmerston—and de Gaulle reached out to French forces throughout the world for support. Once again, the answers were negative. French military commanders in North Africa and the Middle East saw de Gaulle as a tool of the British and preferred to remain loyal to Vichy. The first exceptions were in the Pacific, where the New Hebrides, New Caledonia, and Tahiti came on board. Then, Equatorial and Central Africa followed in late August, the Cameroons, Chad, and the French Congo rallied to de Gaulle, and shortly afterward, Gabon did the same.

This gave de Gaulle a base outside England, and he set up plans to take Dakar, the capital of Senegal and a major French military base on the Atlantic. With de Gaulle on board, a British-French naval force, including a carrier and two battleships, arrived off Dakar on September 23. When de Gaulle addressed the city by radio declaring his "friendly intentions," Vichy forces fired back. The fighting continued for another day, but it was clear that the forces in Dakar were not going to accept de Gaulle. That evening, the Anglo-French naval force withdrew. One battleship had been badly damaged, and a destroyer and two submarines had been sunk. For de Gaulle, the failure of the mission was a terrible blow to his prestige. "The days which followed were cruel to me," he said; "however, it very soon became clear to me that in spite of the reverse, the Free French remained unshakable. Among the men of our expedition . . . not one wished to leave me. On the contrary, all of them had been hardened by the hostile attitude of Vichy."[13]

In London, Churchill defended the operation in the House of Commons. "All that has happened has only strengthened His Majesty's Government in the confidence it extended to General de Gaulle."[14] Nevertheless, many British leaders became skeptical. Lord Halifax, who was still foreign minister, believed Vichy should not be written off. And in the United States, the defeat at Dakar intensified FDR's hostility to de Gaulle. Roosevelt believed the future of France lay with Pétain and Vichy, and in this belief he was strongly supported by Secretary of State Cordell Hull and the State Department. As Undersecretary of State Sumner Welles put it: "De Gaulle's authority is based upon a small group of followers who sometimes fight each other, and on some overseas territories. . . . Eighty-five percent of the French living in the United States are not for de Gaulle."[15] The initial role of the French in the United States in support of Vichy was important in shaping FDR's view. Alexis Léger, former French ambassador to the United States and then secretary general in the French Foreign Office, had retired and come to the United States just before the armistice. He was held in high esteem by Roosevelt and the State Department, and from the beginning was highly critical of General de Gaulle and the Free French movement. These views he shared repeatedly with the U.S. government, and they had an effect.[16]

De Gaulle spent the next six weeks in Equatorial Africa. He received a tumultuous welcome in Douala, the capital of the Cameroons, and on October 27 at Brazzaville in the Congo, he announced the creation of a Committee of Imperial Defence to direct French forces in the war. The British had not been consulted beforehand, and the Committee of Imperial Defence was de Gaulle's first step toward acquiring the status of head of a provisional government. The British Foreign Office was not pleased, but Churchill stood by him. De Gaulle had to be assertive, said the prime minister, "to prove to French eyes that he was not a British puppet."*

De Gaulle returned to England in mid-November. He continued to have warm personal relations with Churchill, often spending the weekend at Chequers, Churchill's country estate. On January 15 he signed an agreement with Anthony Eden, minister of war, defining the status of the Free French on British territory. With British help he also established a bank, the Caisse Centrale

---

* "He certainly carried out this policy with perseverance," said Churchill. "He even one day explained this technique to me, and I fully comprehended the extraordinary difficulties of his problem. I always admired his massive strength." Winston S. Churchill, *Their Finest Hour* (Boston: Houghton Mifflin, 1949), 509.

de la France Libre, to handle financial affairs for the Free French movement, further solidifying his base.

As summer approached, de Gaulle advanced a proposal to re-take the French territories of Syria and Lebanon from Vichy. The outbreak of an anti-British revolt in Iraq, which was a British pro-tectorate, suggested that Germany might take over Syria as a base for helping the Iraqi rebels, and Churchill quickly saw the benefits of de Gaulle's suggestion. The prime minister pressed both the Foreign Office and the military to take action. They were reluc-tant, but complied. Churchill ordered General Archibald Wavell, the area commander, to supply support for the Free French and cabled de Gaulle of his decision. De Gaulle was amazed that Chur-chill was acting so quickly. For the first and only time, he wrote his reply to Churchill in English:

1) Thank you.

2) [General] Castroux will remain in Palestine.

3) I shall go to Cairo soon.

4) You will win the war.[17]

On June 8, 1941, Anglo-French forces, comprised of mostly Free French troops, attacked Syria. As at Dakar, the Vichy forces fought back, but this time the Free French held on, and after four weeks the garrison surrendered. But instead of surrendering to the Free French, the Vichy commander signed an armistice with the British commander, General Maitland Wilson. The Free French were not mentioned. De Gaulle was furious. When he threatened to withdraw his troops from British command, the armistice was amended.

But friction with the British continued. In Brazzaville on August 27, de Gaulle gave an interview to George Weller of the *Chicago Daily News* in which he said England "is carrying on a wartime deal with Hitler in which Vichy serves as a go-between."[18] When the interview was published, Churchill hit the roof. "If de Gaulle's interview with the American press at Brazzaville is authentic," he wrote Anthony Eden, who had succeeded Halifax as foreign minister, "he has clearly gone off his head. This would be a very good riddance and will simplify our further course."[19] Eden, who was one of de Gaulle's major supporters in the government, pointed out the general's importance as a rallying point in France against Vichy, and told Churchill that "if he shows indications of repentance, I hope you will not underestimate your power to complete the cure."[20]

When de Gaulle returned to London at the beginning of September, he was held at arm's length by British officials. After two weeks, Churchill agreed to see him. The meeting began in a frosty tone but quickly became businesslike. The situation in the Middle East was discussed, and Churchill assured de Gaulle that the British had no interest in occupying Syria and that the Free French were in charge. The alliance was back in place. Churchill suggested that de Gaulle establish a formal council to lead the Free French politically, and de Gaulle agreed. The two men ended the meeting with much of their previous warmth restored. Churchill greatly respected de Gaulle's determination to liberate France, and de Gaulle understood that Churchill was one of the few who understood his sense of mission and could help him deliver on it.[21]

De Gaulle's relations with the United States, however, continued to be negative. President Roosevelt considered him "just another French general," and continued to pursue relations with Vichy. The Japanese attack on Pearl Harbor changed nothing. This became evident in late December 1941, when de Gaulle, with Churchill's approval, mounted a takeover of the islands of St. Pierre and Miquelon, just off the coast of Newfoundland. On Christmas Eve, Free French Marines landed at St. Pierre and were received enthusiastically by the local population. A plebiscite in the islands immediately afterward gave the Free French 95 percent support. The Canadian government was pleased and so was Churchill. But in Washington, a storm broke. Roosevelt opposed anything that would alienate the Pétain government, and Secretary of State Hull was livid. Hull issued an immediate communiqué condemning "the arbitrary action" taken by the "so-called Free French," and asking Canada to intervene.[22] Canadian Prime Minister Mackenzie King dismissed Hull's plea, and public opinion in the United States strongly supported de Gaulle's action. Hull received an avalanche of mail addressed to the "so-called Secretary of State," and the affair clearly showed that public opinion in the United States was on de Gaulle's side. At a White House luncheon on New Year's Day, 1942, Churchill joked to FDR, "You're being nice to Vichy, we've been nice to de Gaulle. It's a fair division of labour."[23]

While de Gaulle's relations with Washington continued on a downward slope, Moscow became supportive. On September 26, 1941, with German troops advancing eastward in Russia, the Soviets recognized de Gaulle as the "Leader of all the Free French."[24] At that point the Russians withdrew their ambassador from Vichy and assigned him to de Gaulle in London, and de Gaulle posted an emissary in Moscow. When Soviet foreign minister Vyacheslav Molotov visited London in May 1942, he and de Gaulle had several lengthy discussions. Molotov said that his government was an ally of London and Washington, "but with France, Russia desires to have an independent alliance."[25] The support of the Soviet Union greatly improved de Gaulle's relations with the French Communist Party.

Additional momentum was provided by the Free French troops at Bir Hakeim in Libya in early June. Under the command of General Pierre Koenig, the 5,500 troops of the First Light Division held up Erwin Rommel's much larger Afrika Korps for almost two weeks, allowing the British Eighth Army time to regroup. It was an outstanding performance, made even more so by Koenig's ability to break out after the battle and save his troops from destruction. "To the whole world the guns of Bir Hakeim announced the beginning of the recovery of France," said de Gaulle.[26] Churchill was equally expressive, calling Bir Hakeim "one of the finest feats of arms in this war."[27]

De Gaulle was also moving to solidify his base. Following Churchill's suggestion, he formed an eight-member National

General Pierre Koenig at Bir Hakeim

Committee with himself as chairman. That gave the Free French the appearance of a national government. The National Committee claimed to be "the sole representative of France and the empire," although it was not yet recognized by either Britain or the United States.[28] The Committee met weekly at Free French headquarters on Carlton Gardens, and as de Gaulle said, "No important step was ever taken without the Committee having deliberated it first."[29]

But de Gaulle was still very much in the wilderness. When American troops landed in the French territories of Morocco and Algeria in November 1942, de Gaulle was not informed beforehand. This was Roosevelt's personal decision. FDR despised de Gaulle and believed he was a phony. Roosevelt also insisted that the landing be made initially by American troops, believing that the presence of British forces would encourage the Vichy troops to resist. To encourage their cooperation, the Americans enlisted General Henri Giraud, a four-star French general with a distinguished combat record who had escaped German captivity and was living quietly in the Loire. A supporter of the Pétain government, he became FDR's choice as an alternative to de Gaulle, and someone who could win over the Vichy garrisons in Algeria and Morocco without a fight.[30] But it was a bad choice. Giraud was over his head. He was totally unfamiliar with the situation in North Africa. As Eisenhower said later, Giraud "wanted to be a big shot, a bright and shining light, and the acclaimed savior of France, but turned out to be a terrible blow to our expectations."[31]

When the Americans encountered stiff resistance from Vichy's forces, they turned to Admiral Jean Darlan, Pétain's deputy, who was in Algiers visiting his son, who was ill with polio. The American high command quickly reached an agreement with Darlan. Vichy forces would stop fighting in Morocco and Algeria, and in return Darlan would become high commissioner of North Africa and Giraud the commander of all French forces there. Once again, de Gaulle was excluded.

Churchill did his best to reassure de Gaulle, and placed the blame for his exclusion on the United States. "We have been obliged to go along with this," said the prime minister, but "rest assured, we are not revoking any of our agreements with you. . . . You have been with us during the worst moments of the war. We shall not abandon you now that the horizon is brightening." [32]

To Roosevelt, Churchill cabled, "I ought to let you know that very deep currents of feeling are stirred by the arrangement with Darlan. The more I reflect upon it the more convinced I become that it can only be a temporary expedient, justifiable solely by the stress of battle." [33]

The American decision to install Darlan as high commissioner in North Africa may have saved a few American lives, but it kept in place the most despicable aspects of the Vichy regime. Pétain was still recognized as leader, Nazi sympathizers remained in office, Jews continued to be persecuted, and the Gaullist symbol, the Cross of Lorraine, continued to be banned. The situation changed dramatically on Christmas Eve 1942, when Darlan was assassinated. Exactly who organized his killing has never been determined. White House officials insisted the assassin was a Gaullist, but numerous investigations have shown that the weapon used was provided by a member of the OSS.* Roosevelt insisted that Darlan be replaced by General Giraud. De Gaulle did not protest. But the tide was turning. Giraud was obviously not capable of

---

* Darlan's assassin was being trained in the Corps France d'Afrique under the direction of Carleton S. Coon, a peacetime professor of anthropology at Harvard, and the resident Office of Strategic Services officer in the area. The weapon the assassin used was a Colt Woodsman pistol, identical to the one owned by Coon. Immediately after the assassination, Coon was transferred to a British unit in Tunisia. See Jean Edward Smith, *Eisenhower in War and Peace* (New York: Random House, 2012), 251.

managing the political situation. As historian Antony Beevor has pointed out, Roosevelt's policy in North Africa may have worked to de Gaulle's advantage. "American support for Darlan and then Giraud provided the stepping stones from Vichy to Free France, thus averting the danger of civil war in French North Africa."[34]

But the path was not easy. The Casablanca Conference between Roosevelt and Churchill in January 1943 looked initially like another setback. Both leaders were eager to bring de Gaulle and Giraud together and put the Free French under Giraud's control. They therefore invited both men to Casablanca. "We'll call Giraud the bridegroom, and I bring him from Algeria," FDR cabled Churchill, "and you bring the bride, de Gaulle, down from London, and we will have a shotgun wedding."[35] De Gaulle reluctantly came to the conference, but he did not agree to put the Free French under Giraud's control. He and Giraud met, and de Gaulle agreed to pose for pictures with FDR, Churchill, and Giraud, but he did not agree to sign a document prepared by Roosevelt and Churchill that would have effectively eliminated the Free French as the repository of France's sovereignty. Churchill was furious. "Of all our encounters during the war," said de Gaulle, "this was the most ungracious." De Gaulle also saw Roosevelt. "My reception at his hands was a skillful one—that is, kind of sorrowful."[36]

Before leaving the conference, de Gaulle drafted a short communiqué that he and Giraud signed, in which they said, "We have seen each other. We have spoken together." The communiqué went on to affirm their belief in the ultimate victory of France, and most importantly established a permanent liaison group.[37] The establishment of the liaison group turned out to be a great victory for de Gaulle because it began the process of bringing Free France to North Africa.

The next four months may have been de Gaulle's most difficult. Roosevelt and the State Department intensified their campaign

At Casablanca in January 1943.
Left to right: Giraud, FDR, de Gaulle, Churchill.

against him, and Churchill—always eager to ingratiate himself with FDR—went along. In Washington for a conference with the president, Churchill cabled Eden on May 22 telling him to ask the cabinet to revoke the 1940 agreement with de Gaulle. "He hates England and has left a trail of Anglophobia behind him everywhere. . . . I beg that you will bring this before the Cabinet at the earliest moment." [38] Eden submitted Churchill's request to the cabinet that evening and it was unanimously rejected. As Eden wrote in his diary, "Cabinet at 9 p.m. re de Gaulle and Winston's proposed to break with him now. Everyone against and very brave about it in his absence." [39]

The fact is, de Gaulle now held the winning hand. Public opinion in North Africa, France, Britain, and the United States was strongly on his side, and in the fighting in Tunisia, Free French forces had done surprisingly well. Even more important, the resistance in France was coming together. De Gaulle's appeal spanned the political spectrum, from the Communist left to the monarchical right. His representative in France, Jean Moulin, had worked hard to bring the factions together, and on May 15 he told de Gaulle that a National Council of the Resistance (CNR) had been formed and that it strongly endorsed him "as the unquestioned leader."* Meeting clandestinely for the first time in Paris on May 27, the council recognized de Gaulle as the leader of the Resistance and demanded that he be installed as president of a French provisional government.

In Algeria, Giraud recognized the inevitable. In late May, he invited de Gaulle to come to Algiers and form a government with him. De Gaulle accepted. "I plan to reach Algiers by the end of this week, and I shall be delighted to work directly with you in the service of France."[40] On May 30, de Gaulle landed in Algiers. Unlike his arrival at Casablanca, this time General Giraud was at the airport, a French honor guard presented arms, and a French band played *La Marseillaise.* Four days later Giraud and de Gaulle reached agreement. A French Committee of National Liberation (FCNL) was formed and de Gaulle and Giraud became co-presidents. The committee proclaimed itself "the central French power. It directs the French war effort. . . . It exercises French sovereignty."[41] Equally important, several Vichyite office holders in North Africa retired, and their replacements were Free French. De Gaulle was received by the population of Algiers with a wave of popular demonstrations involving all classes and all political persuasions.

---

* The National Council of the Resistance had sixteen members: eight from the Resistance movements in France, five from political parties (Socialist, Communist, Radical, Republican Federation, and Democratic Alliance), two from trade unions (CGT and CFTC), and Moulin as chairman.

De Gaulle and Giraud in Algeria

Roosevelt was appalled by the creation of the FCNL and immediately set about to destroy de Gaulle's position. "I am fed up
with de Gaulle," he cabled Churchill on June 17. "The time has
arrived when we must break him."[42] On the same day, FDR told
Eisenhower, "It is important that you should know for your very
secret information that we may possibly break with de Gaulle in
the next few days."[43] Roosevelt had allowed his personal antago-
nism to de Gaulle to obscure the reality of the situation. In July he
invited Giraud to the United States for what he assumed would
be a ceremonial laying on of hands. Giraud was received unen-
thusiastically by the North American audience, and by the time
he returned to Algiers at the end of the month, de Gaulle had secured his position as the sole president of the FCNL, which had
become the de facto government of France in exile. De Gaulle was
adept at taking advantage of Giraud's absence, and he was warmly

embraced by the other members of the FCNL. De Gaulle captured the change when he described his return to Casablanca in August: "Six months before I had to reside on the city's outskirts, constrained to secrecy and surrounded with barbed wire and American sentry posts. Today my presence served as a symbol and a center of French authority."[44]

Belated recognition of the FCNL came at the Quebec Conference between Churchill and Roosevelt in late August. Churchill had come to recognize that de Gaulle was in charge and that the FCNL was effectively the government of France in exile. The Soviet Union had officially recognized the FCNL in July, and it was time for Britain and the United States to do the same. In the end, both countries issued statements at Quebec recognizing the FCNL, although the American statement was much more limited. "The government of the United States recognizes the French Committee of National Liberation as administering the French overseas territories which acknowledge its authority. This statement does not constitute recognition of a government of France or of the French Empire by the government of the United States."[45]

For all practical purposes, de Gaulle was now the undisputed leader of France's exile government. On September 12, 1943, the FCNL created a Provisional Consultative Assembly, which was the beginning of a genuinely representative government, and de Gaulle was again overwhelmingly endorsed. By December, the military forces of the Free French under his command numbered more than 400,000, and four divisions, led by General Alphonse Juin, were already fighting on the Allied side in Italy. The Resistance in France was also supportive, and de Gaulle continued his efforts to bring it together. Jean Moulin, his original Resistance leader, had been captured by the Germans and tortured to death. De Gaulle appointed Alexandre Parodi to succeed him and shortly afterward named General Pierre Koenig, the hero of Bir Hakeim, to command the French Forces of the Interior (FFI)—the Resistance forces acting within France. Koenig was based in London, but his command was all-encompassing. The French Communist Party also rallied round, and was rewarded with three seats on the FCNL.

Churchill made peace as well. Returning from the Tehran Conference with Roosevelt and Stalin, the prime minister met de Gaulle in Marrakesh, Morocco. Once again the meeting began frosty but quickly warmed up. Churchill said he regretted the conflict that had arisen between them and that England and France must work together. De Gaulle agreed. Churchill then asked whether Franco-British friendship would extend into the postwar period. "France will be exhausted after this terrible ordeal," de Gaulle replied, "and to recover she will need help from all quarters, especially from the United States and Great Britain." Churchill was pleased. "If this is so," he told de Gaulle, "we should deal gently with each other." [46]

De Gaulle invited Churchill to join him at a military review the next day, and Churchill accepted. The review was a major success. According to de Gaulle, "The ceremony took place amid the liveliest popular enthusiasm. For the crowd in Marrakesh, and for those everywhere else who would see the newsreels . . . the appearance of Churchill and de Gaulle side by side signified that the Allied armies would soon be together in victory." [47]

General Dwight D. Eisenhower, commanding Allied forces in North Africa, was even more pleased by de Gaulle's achievement. Throughout the North African campaign Ike had had to deal with Darlan and Giraud, and neither was capable of governing the area. But de Gaulle and the FCNL did a superb job. And with the invasion of France pending, Eisenhower was convinced that de Gaulle was essential. Accordingly, on December 30, 1943, just before leaving for Washington and London, where he would become supreme commander of the Allied invasion, Eisenhower requested an appointment and then called on de Gaulle at his office.

"You were originally described to me in an unfavorable sense," said Eisenhower. "Today I recognize that that judgment was in error. For the coming battle, I shall need not only the cooperation of your forces, but still more the assistance of your officials and the moral support of the French people. I must have your assistance and I have come to ask for it."

"Splendid," de Gaulle replied. "You are a man! For you know how to say, 'I was wrong.'"[48]

According to Ike, the meeting became "a love feast."[49] De Gaulle raised the question of the liberation of Paris and said, "It must be with French troops." Eisenhower agreed, and it was decided to send a French division under General Jacques-Philippe Leclerc to England as soon as possible. As Ike prepared to leave, he told de Gaulle he did not know what "theoretical position" Washington would take, but "I can assure you that as far as I am concerned I will recognize no French power in France other than your own."[50]

The Allies Advance

"He and I were never Charles and Ike. Never. . . . He's rather remote and I think he believes his position requires it. . . . But there was always a good feeling; not only of respect and admiration, but a very measurable degree of affection."

—EISENHOWER ON DE GAULLE, AUGUST 25, 1964

E isenhower and de Gaulle understood each other. They were the same age, born within a month of each other in 1890. Both came from large families that were very religious, both attended their country's military academy, and both had spent their early careers commanding tank units. Both read assiduously, wrote well, and possessed a remarkable command of their respective languages. Each identified with his country's heritage, and in many respects exemplified its virtues. De Gaulle's war record was exceptional, and Eisenhower respected it. Wounded three times on the Western Front in World War I, he was left for dead on the battlefield only to be rescued and healed by the Germans.

De Gaulle also recognized and appreciated the position in which Eisenhower had been placed. "If occasionally he went so far as to support the pretexts which tended to keep us in obscurity, I can affirm he did so without conviction. I even saw him submit to my intervention in his own strategy whenever national interest led me to do so. At least this great soldier felt, in his turn, that mysterious sympathy which for almost two centuries had brought his country and mine together in the world's great dramas."[1]

The first area where cooperation between de Gaulle and Eisenhower was essential was in overriding the instructions from Roosevelt and the State Department pertaining to liberated France. When Ike arrived in London in January 1944, he was informed by his chief of staff Walter Bedell Smith that the State Department had instructed Allied headquarters to have no dealings with the French Committee of National Liberation (FCNL) or de Gaulle pertaining to civil affairs in France. Washington had established a School of Military Government at the University of Virginia in 1942 to train officers to manage civil affairs in former enemy-occupied countries. This produced the American Military Government in Occupied Territories (AMGOT), which was already in operation in Italy, and Roosevelt was adamant that it should also take over France when the Germans were pushed out.

Eisenhower was dumbfounded. As he saw it, there was no alternative to de Gaulle and the FCNL. Roosevelt's instructions had to be overturned. On January 15, Ike cabled General George Marshall in the War Department. "It is essential that immediate crystallization of plans relating to civil affairs in Metropolitan France be accomplished. This requires conferences with properly accredited French authorities. I assume, of course, that such authorities will be representatives of the Committee of National Liberation. I therefore request that General de Gaulle be asked to designate an individual or group of individuals with whom I can enter into immediate negotiations in London. The need for prompt action cannot be overemphasized, since we will desire to turn over to French control at the earliest possible date those areas that are not essential for military operations."[2]

Eisenhower's cable was a frontal assault on FDR's plan. The

War Department was sympathetic, and Assistant Secretary of War John J. McCloy was dispatched to convince Roosevelt of Eisenhower's need for de Gaulle. McCloy, former managing partner of the prestigious New York law firm of Cravath, Swaine & Moore, was a favorite of FDR, and after thirty minutes of subtle flattery he brought the president to accept what Ike was doing. Roosevelt authorized McCloy to tell Eisenhower "informally" that he should feel free in making decisions about French civil affairs, "even if it involved dealing with representatives of the French Committee."[3] McCloy kept at it, and two months later Roosevelt approved a War Department directive that empowered Eisenhower to decide "when, where, and how the Civil Administration in France" would be conducted. Eisenhower was given explicit authority to consult with the FCNL and allow it to select and install civil officers, providing this did not constitute official recognition of the committee as the government of France.[4]

For Eisenhower, the issue was over and he had won. "The whole matter has been thrown back in my lap," he noted in a memorandum, "and I may deal with any French body that seems capable of assisting us."[5] De Gaulle was less pleased but understood. "Actually, the President's intentions seemed to me on the same order as Alice's Adventures in Wonderland. In North Africa, Roosevelt had already ventured on a political enterprise analogous to the one he was now contemplating for France. Yet of that attempt nothing remained. . . . That the failure of his policy in Africa had not been able to dispel Roosevelt's illusions was a situation I regretted for him and for our relations."[6]

As D-Day approached, Roosevelt began to hedge his authorization, and Eisenhower again went to the mat. Writing to the Combined Chiefs of Staff on May 11, Ike said, "The limitations under which we are operating in dealing with the French are becoming very embarrassing and are producing a situation that is becoming very dangerous. We began our military discussions with the French representatives here in the belief that, although we have no formal directive, we understood the policies of our government well enough to be able to reach a working way with any French body or organization that can effectively assist us in the fight against Germany. For the present there is no such body represented here except the French Committee of National Liberation." Eisenhower told the Combined Chiefs it was increasingly urgent to resolve a host of issues pertaining to the upcoming situation in liberated France. "The most effective means of doing so would be for General de Gaulle himself to come to London. I would then be able to deal with him direct on the most immediate and pressing problems of the initial approach to the French people and their organized resistance groups."[7]

Churchill agreed with Eisenhower that de Gaulle should come to London, but again FDR resisted. In the president's view, there must be no discussion of political affairs in France with de Gaulle. "I know you will understand that any matters relating to the future government of France are a political and not a military matter," Roosevelt told Eisenhower. "We must always remember that the French population is quite naturally shell-shocked. . . . It will take some time for them to quietly and normally think through matters pertaining to their political future. We as liberators have no 'right' to color their views or give any group the sole right to impose one side of a case on them."[8] Roosevelt was gearing up to run for a fourth term and his health was failing.* He was also supported in his hostility to de Gaulle by the senior level in the State

---

* Roosevelt's health began to fail badly in early 1944. When he died in April 1945, his medical records, including all clinical notes and test results, were immediately destroyed by Admiral Ross McIntire, his personal physician. Jean Edward Smith, *FDR* (New York: Random House, 2007), 602–607.

Department who were still enthralled by Vichy, and by the daily anti–de Gaulle rants of Admiral Leahy, FDR's former ambassador to Pétain who was now the chairman of the Joint Chiefs of Staff, with his office in the White House.

Eisenhower was taken aback by Roosevelt's resistance. On May 16, he cabled FDR, "you may be quite certain that my dealings with the French Committee will be confined to military matters and related civil administration. . . . I understand your anxiety in the matter and I assure you that I will carefully avoid anything that could be interpreted as an effort to influence the character of the future government of France. However, I think I should tell you that so far as I am able to determine from information given to me through agents and through escaped prisoners of war, there exists in France today only two major groups, of which one is the Vichy gang, and the other characterized by unreasoning admiration of de Gaulle." Eisenhower told FDR that once ashore he expected to find "a universal desire to adhere to the Gaullist group."

Eisenhower was counting on Roosevelt's ultimate willingness to defer to the commander in the field. But as a backstop, he reminded the president that SHAEF (Supreme Headquarters Allied Expeditionary Force) was an Allied command. "I hope that your desires on this subject of which I am already aware, can eventually come to me as a joint directive of the two governments." [9] By suggesting that Roosevelt needed British approval, Eisenhower was providing himself with some wiggle room.

As supreme commander, Eisenhower knew that he needed de Gaulle, and he had already given him his promise of support. "We were depending on considerable assistance from the Resistance in France, and an open clash with de Gaulle would hurt us immeasurably," Ike wrote in his memoirs. Roosevelt was a problem and would have to be dealt with. As Eisenhower saw it, "de Gaulle would represent the only authority that could produce any kind of French coordination and unification, and no harm would result from giving him the kind of recognition he sought. He would merely be placed on notice that once the country was liberated the freely expressed will of the French people would determine their own government." [10]

Eisenhower did his utmost to maintain his ties to de Gaulle. On May 23 he wrote the general to congratulate him on the performance of Free French troops in Italy under General Alphonse Juin. "Although I have never for one minute doubted that the reborn French Army would distinguish itself from the first moment of its entry into battle, and on this basis have consistently urged the rearming of the French divisions, it is most gratifying to me as it must be to you to have our faith confirmed in this striking and spectacular manner." [11] (On May 14, 1944, General Juin's troops broke through the German "Gustav Line" on the river Garigliano, forcing the Germans to withdraw northward.)

De Gaulle's response was exactly what Ike had hoped for. "I assure you again that the French government is very happy to have a place in your army under your supreme command for operations in the Western theater, and it has the fullest confidence that you will conduct the armies of liberation to a rapid and complete victory." [12]

On May 26—less than two weeks before D-Day—the Committee of National Liberation in Algiers declared itself the Provisional Government of the French Republic, with de Gaulle at its head. That same day Churchill cabled FDR: "It is very difficult to cut the French out of the liberation of France," and he requested the president's acquiescence to inviting de Gaulle to London. [13] Roosevelt reluctantly agreed. "I hope your conversations with General de Gaulle will persuade him to contribute to the liberation of France without imposing his authority over the French people." [14]

Churchill sent his personal plane to Algiers to fetch de Gaulle, who arrived in London on June 4. The prime minister immediately took him to Ike's field headquarters near Portsmouth, where, Churchill told Roosevelt, "Generals Eisenhower and Bedell Smith went to their utmost limit in their endeavor to conciliate him, making it clear that in practice events would probably mean that the Committee [FCNL] would be the natural authority with whom the Supreme Commander would deal." [15] Churchill was preparing FDR for what would become the new reality in France.

Eisenhower gave de Gaulle a lengthy briefing on Operation Overlord, the planned Allied landings in Normandy. Then it was agreed that General Pierre Koenig would fold the Resistance (FFI) into the French army and report to Ike. Eisenhower told de Gaulle he was worried about the weather, and had at most twenty-four hours to decide on a date for the landing. "What do you think I should do?"

De Gaulle, who was flattered that Ike had asked him, insisted the decision was Eisenhower's alone. "Whatever decision you make, I approve in advance and without reservation. I will only tell you that in your place I should not delay." [16]

When the briefing concluded, Eisenhower, with evident embarrassment, gave de Gaulle a speech, written by speechwriters at SHAEF, that they wanted de Gaulle to deliver to France after the troops had landed. As Ike had anticipated, de Gaulle refused. Instead, he wrote his own:

> The supreme battle has been joined. . . . It is, of course, the Battle of France, and the battle for France! For the sons of France, wherever they are, whatever they are, the simple and sacred duty is to fight the enemy by every means in their power. . . . The orders given by the French government and by the leaders it has recognized must be followed precisely. . . . From behind the cloud so heavy with our blood and our tears, the sun of our greatness is now reappearing. [17]

Eisenhower was delighted. De Gaulle did not say he was the president of France nor did he call Ike the supreme commander, but it was obvious what he meant. To the Combined Chiefs, Ike cabled, "General de Gaulle and his chief of staff are anxious to assist every possible way and to have the lodgments effected as soon as possible."[18]

With the landing of 155,000 Allied troops on June 6, Eisenhower took charge. And the relationship with de Gaulle prospered. Behind the scenes, Ike had sent an explicit directive on May 25 to the British and American commanders who would land on D-Day: "Military government will *not* be established in liberated France. . . . The French themselves will conduct all aspects of civil administration in their country, even in areas of military operations."[19]

On June 14, little more than a week after the Allies had landed, de Gaulle returned to France with a lightning visit to the ancient Norman city of Bayeux, famous for its tapestry depicting the Battle of Hastings, where the Normans defeated the Anglo-Saxons. Bayeux was the first French city liberated by the Allies, and de Gaulle's return was a spectacular event. He dismounted from his vehicle and proceeded on foot to the town hall. He was immediately surrounded by cheering crowds. "We walked on together, all overwhelmed by comradeship, feeling national joy, pride, and hope rise again from the depths of the abyss," he later wrote.[20] De Gaulle also visited two nearby towns, received similar receptions, and departed that evening feeling in control. Whatever doubts Washington may have had about the general's support had been overwhelmingly dispelled. And for all practical purposes, Bayeux had become the temporary capital of liberated France.

De Gaulle returned to Algiers on June 16, addressed the French Consultative Assembly (the temporary stand-in for the National Assembly), informed them of what had been achieved, and paid special tribute to Eisenhower, "in whom the French Government has complete confidence for the victorious conduct of the common military operations."[21] As de Gaulle recognized, it was Ike who was primarily responsible for the swift transition he had made from being an outcast to being the leader of France. Eisenhower had ignored Washington's wishes and relied on his own judgment. Having suffered through the chaos of civil affairs in North Africa, he was not about to let it happen again.

De Gaulle's lightning visit to Bayeux established the Provisional Government of the French Republic in Normandy. De Gaulle appointed François Coulet as regional commissioner, and Coulet moved quickly to consolidate his position. Roosevelt, at a press conference in Washington on June 23, once again attempted to debunk the effort. "Let us liberate a little more of France before we go into the matter of civil administration," said the president, but it was clear that the liberated territory welcomed de Gaulle's representatives.[22] As Anthony Eden put it, "Whatever de Gaulle's gifts or failings, he was a godsend to his country at this hour, when France must otherwise have been distracted by controversy or bathed in blood."[23]

Initially, Allied progress was slow. At the end of June, American and British forces had moved little beyond their initial beachhead, and the Germans were holding firm. The Allied buildup continued through July, and on July 26, the breakthrough came when the American VII Corps overwhelmed the German lines at Saint-Lô. George Patton's Third Army tore through the gap in the German lines, and the breakthrough became a breakout. "The whole Western Front has been ripped open," Field Marshal Günther von Kluge, the German commander, informed Berlin. "The left flank has collapsed."[24]

Patton's army raced into Brittany virtually unchecked. "Once a gap appears in the enemy front we must pass into it into the enemy rear areas," said General Bernard Montgomery, who was commanding all Allied ground forces at the time. "The broad strategy of the Allied armies is to swing the right flank towards Paris and force the enemy back to the Seine."[25] In the next three days, Patton advanced one hundred miles, and the Germans now faced encirclement as the Canadian First Army came on from the north.

On August 7, Eisenhower moved his command post from England to the Norman village of Tournières, about twelve miles southwest of Bayeux. The ground war was divided into two army groups—the Twenty-First under Field Marshal Bernard Montgomery, consisting of the Second British Army and the First Canadian Army, and the Twelfth under General Omar Bradley, consisting of the First and Third U.S. armies. "If we can destroy a good portion of the enemy's army now in front of us we will have a greater freedom of movement in northern France and I would expect to move very rapidly," Eisenhower cabled Marshall on August 11.[26]

Kluge and his commanders planned to fall back to a shorter defense line roughly along the Seine, but Hitler rejected the plan and ordered an all-out counterattack at Mortain, the shoulder of the Third Army's breakout. If the German attack was successful, Patton's armored columns would be cut off. But the heroic stand of the U.S. Thirtieth Division at Mortain, combined with round-the-clock air bombardment, saved the day. After a week of some of the heaviest fighting of the war, the Germans found themselves encircled in the Falaise Pocket, the First Canadian Army coming in from the north, and the French Second Armored Division, commanded by Major General Jacques Leclerc, coming in from the south. Jacques Leclerc was the nom de guerre of the Viscount Jacques-Philippe de Hauteclocque, a career French Army officer who had joined de Gaulle in 1940 and had assumed the pseudonym "Leclerc" to protect his family in France. A legendary battlefield commander, Leclerc was most famous for fighting his way north with a Free French force 420 miles from Fort Lamy in Chad to join the British Eighth Army in the Sahara in February 1941.[27]

The French Second Armored Division was unique in many respects. It had been sent to England from Algeria in April 1944 following de Gaulle's earlier discussion with Eisenhower, and was intended to lead the Allies in the liberation of Paris when the time came. Unlike the Free French forces that were fighting in Italy under General Juin, or the First French Army that would soon land on the Riviera, both of which were primarily African troops, the French Second Armored Division under Leclerc was comprised of native Frenchmen, a smattering of European legionnaires (Spanish, Italian, Czech, and Polish), plus a Chadian regiment and a battalion of Moroccan Spahis. It was organized to

General Leclerc

make the best possible impression in Paris, and Leclerc was an ideal commander for that purpose.

The battlefield at the Falaise Pocket was one of the fiercest killing grounds of the war in the west. "Forty-eight hours after the closing of the gap," Eisenhower wrote in his memoirs, "I was conducted through it on foot; to encounter scenes that could only be described by Dante. It was literally possible to walk for hundreds of yards at a time, stepping on nothing but dead and decaying flesh."[28]

The battle for Normandy was over. It had raged for seventy-five days. The Germans had deployed 600,000 men and 1,500 tanks, commanded initially by Field Marshals von Rundstedt and Rommel, then by Kluge. The Allies also deployed about 600,000 men, and 3,000 tanks. The principal difference was the number of planes available. The Allies brought more than 12,000 aircraft to the battle; the Germans had almost none. When the fighting ended, the Germans had lost almost 500,000 men killed, wounded, or captured, and virtually all of their equipment. The Allies lost almost 200,000 men, two-thirds of whom were American.[29] Allied losses were replenished quickly. German losses were irreplaceable.

As German resistance faded, the Allies moved quickly. Patton continued his relentless advance toward the Seine. Le Mans, Orléans, and Chartres fell to the Third Army as the Germans retreated. On August 19, the day the gap on the Falaise Pocket closed, Third Army troops reached the Seine, thirty-fives miles west of Paris, and established a bridgehead on the other side of the river.

Eisenhower's plans called for Paris to be bypassed. Patton's Third Army would swing south of the city, cross the Seine at Melun, near Fontainebleau, and move eastward toward Metz and the German border. The American First Army, commanded by

General Courtney Hodges, would move north of the city heading for Reims, the Ardennes, and Luxembourg. General Montgomery's Twenty-First Army Group would assault the V-1 and V-2 rocket launching sites in the Pas-de-Calais, move into Belgium, and take the port of Antwerp.

Eisenhower believed Paris should be entered at a later date. If the Germans defended the city, street fighting would consume the Allies for a month. Casualties would be high and the collateral damage would be unacceptable. At present, Paris was undamaged, and air raids had only hit the suburbs. There was also a serious logistical problem that Ike wished to avoid. Providing food and fuel for a city of four million people would strain Allied supply lines to the breaking point. General Pierre Koenig, commanding the French Forces of the Interior, had ordered the Paris Resistance to stand down until notified, and Eisenhower was confident the Allies could bypass Paris for the moment.

De Gaulle watched the Allied advance from Algiers. In early July, FDR had invited him to Washington and had provided a plane to fly him to the nation's capital. De Gaulle arrived on July 6 and stayed five days, also going to New York and Canada, where he was warmly received. With the American election under way, the trip was Roosevelt's way of putting the issue of de Gaulle and the FCNL behind him. The press and the public were enthusiastic. De Gaulle was also on his best behavior. When he returned to Algiers on July 13, he received a message from Washington that should have put matters to rest. "The United States recognizes that the French Committee of National Liberation is competent to insure the administration of France." [30]

Back in Algiers, de Gaulle asked the Resistance to stand down until the Allies were ready. On August 11 he wrote a new "directive to the Resistance" that was very cautious:

For Paris and the great occupied cities

1. Do not carry out tasks useful to the enemy; if the enemy tries to enforce them, go on strike.

2. If the enemy weakens, seize his employees in the factory, whatever their jobs may be. Use them as hostages.

3. In any event, prevent the retreating enemy from taking his staff and machines with him.

4. Return to work at once and in an orderly manner as soon as the Allied forces move.[31]

Three days later he sent a telegram to FDR telling him that according to reports he was receiving from France, "it will be possible to establish order there without any great upheaval."[32] But the situation in Paris changed quickly. And de Gaulle, like Eisenhower, was caught off guard. On August 12, French railway workers walked off the job, paralyzing the city's transportation net. On the fifteenth, the Paris police force went on strike. On the eighteenth, the postal service shut down, the Communist newspaper *L'Humanité* called for a popular insurrection, and three thousand policemen, armed but wearing civilian clothes, seized the *préfecture de police* and raised the French flag, the *tricolore*.

De Gaulle monitored the changing situation closely. He was concerned that the Communists might be attempting to seize power. "If they managed to establish themselves as directors of the uprising and to control the authority in Paris, they could easily establish a *de facto* government there in which they would be preponderant."[33] To meet the threat, he decided to take charge personally. On August 14 de Gaulle advised General "Jumbo"

Wilson, the overall Allied commander in the Mediterranean, that he wished to return to France in the next day or two. (The trip still required Allied approval.) Wilson forwarded de Gaulle's request to Eisenhower, who told the Combined Chiefs of Staff he had no objection, and that he thought de Gaulle wanted to be present at the liberation of Paris. Eisenhower asked whether de Gaulle's "rather premature arrival will in any way embarrass the British or American governments." [34]

At the War Department, Eisenhower's query was fielded by John McCloy, who raised no objection. Neither the White House nor the State Department was informed. The British were more than eager for de Gaulle to return because they too were already worried about the possibility of a Communist insurrection in Paris.[35] One problem was that de Gaulle wanted to return to France in a French plane. Ike offered an American B-17, but de Gaulle insisted on using his own aircraft, an unarmed Lockheed Lodestar. He took off from Algiers on the afternoon of August 18, bound for Casablanca. He was accompanied by General Juin and a host of officers using the B-17 the Americans had provided. De Gaulle intended to stop only briefly in Casablanca but mechanical problems in the accompanying B-17 required him to spend the night there.

On the morning of the nineteenth he left Casablanca for Gibraltar, before proceeding up the coast of Spain and France. In Gibraltar, the B-17 developed more mechanical problems, and de Gaulle was told it would be best to wait until they were repaired, rather than proceed alone. He rejected the advice and took off in his Lodestar on schedule. Approaching Normandy at night in heavy weather, his pilot, Colonel de Marmier, became disoriented and wound up flying over England. The plane was low on fuel, but de Gaulle refused de Marmier permission to land in the United Kingdom and refuel. Instead, he joined Marmier in the cockpit and directed the plane back across the Channel. When the plane touched down at Maupertuis, near Cherbourg, just after eight on the morning of August 20, the fuel gauge read empty. Despite the problems, de Gaulle had made the trip successfully. He was met when he landed by General Koenig and François Coulet, the commissioner of the republic in Normandy, as well as an officer from Eisenhower's headquarters who was assigned to bring de Gaulle to meet with Ike as soon as possible.

De Gaulle arrived at Eisenhower's headquarters in Tournières shortly after 10 a.m. on August 20. The men greeted each other warmly. De Gaulle congratulated Ike on "the astonishing speed of the Allied forces' success," and then listened intently as the supreme commander explained his plans for the coming advance.[36] Patton's Third Army would cross the Seine at Mantes north of Paris and at Melun to the south, while Montgomery advanced toward Rouen and the Belgian frontier. Patton would then move toward Lorraine, where he would link up with the armies of General Jean de Lattre de Tassigny and General Alexander Patch coming up from the Mediterranean and solidify the front. De Gaulle was impressed with the thoroughness of Eisenhower's plan, but raised a major concern.

"I don't see why you cross the Seine at Melun, at Mantes, at Rouen—in short, everywhere—and yet at Paris and Paris alone you do not. . . . If any location except the capital of France were in question, my advice would not commit you to any action, for normally the conduct of operations must proceed from you. But the fate of Paris is of fundamental concern to the French government. Which is why I find myself obliged to intervene and to ask you to send French troops there. The French 2nd Armored Division is the obvious choice."[37]

According to de Gaulle, "Eisenhower did not conceal his embarrassment from me. I had the sense that fundamentally he

Ike and de Gaulle at Eisenhower's headquarters

shared my point of view, that he was eager to send Leclerc to Paris, but that for reasons not entirely of a strategic nature he could not yet do so." [38] Those reasons, de Gaulle thought, pertained to what was another effort by the White House and the State Department to short-circuit the FCNL and conclude a separate peace with Pierre Laval and the Vichy government. The problems posed by a Communist takeover led by the Resistance in Paris were clear. What was under the surface were the efforts by Laval to surrender Paris to the Allies with a deal similar to Darlan's in North Africa that would keep Vichy in charge. As de Gaulle put it in his memoirs, "Eisenhower's uncertainty suggested to me that the military command found itself somewhat hampered by the political project pursued by Laval, favored by Roosevelt, and requiring that Paris be protected from all upheavals." De Gaulle wrote that General Juin, visiting Allied headquarters, came to the same conclusions "drawn from his contacts with the general staff." [39]

What Laval proposed is a matter of record. He would convene the French National Assembly, which had not met since 1940, and officially welcome the Allies to Paris. Direct military rule would thus be established through local Vichy officials. Allen Dulles, heading OSS efforts in Bern, Switzerland, was in contact with Laval, as was the American embassy in Madrid. How much the White House was involved has never been proven. French historians tend to accept de Gaulle's version; others are skeptical. [40] Ultimately the plot imploded when Laval could find no French notables to support him.

De Gaulle may be overstating the issue, but it is clear that he believed Laval was planning a coup. He also noted the Resistance activity in Paris and suggested that timely Allied intervention was essential. When Ike said the Resistance had started fighting too soon, de Gaulle met the charge directly. "Why too soon, since at this very moment your forces are on the Seine?" [41] The relationship between de Gaulle and Eisenhower was always warm. Ike acknowledged the problem, and assured de Gaulle that while he could not establish an exact date, he would shortly order Leclerc's division to march on Paris. In his memoirs de Gaulle said he found Washington's policy "quite depressing," but was reassured by Eisenhower's presence. [42]

The following day de Gaulle wrote Eisenhower pressing him once more to move on Paris. "The information which I received today from Paris leads me to believe that owing to the nearly complete disappearance of the police force and the German forces from Paris, the present extreme shortage of food that exists, that serious trouble must be foreseen in the Capital within a short time. I believe that it is really necessary to occupy Paris as soon as possible with French and Allied forces, even if it should produce some fighting and some damage within the city."

De Gaulle said he was sending General Koenig to confer with Eisenhower "on the question of occupation in case you decide to proceed without delay."[43] De Gaulle understood Eisenhower and anticipated that the supreme commander's decision to take Paris would be coming shortly.

— IV —

The German Defense

"The loss of Paris always means the loss of France."

—ADOLF HITLER, AUGUST 23, 1944

The German army in France was in disarray. With a large portion surrounded in the Falaise Pocket, and with General Patton's troops moving toward the Seine, defeat seemed imminent. To complicate matters further, Field Marshal Günther von Kluge, the overall commander, had been ordered back to Berlin to answer questions about the July 20 plot to kill Hitler. Kluge was close to Hitler, but he was also close to the plotters of the assassination attempt, and his possible role was being investigated. The plot to assassinate Hitler was long-standing. Many German generals were involved, and the attempt failed at the last minute when the briefcase with the bomb was moved from where Hitler was sitting and put down on the table. When it exploded, the table saved Hitler. Kluge was relieved of command on August 17, almost a month after the failed coup, and on August 19, while driving back to Germany, he committed suicide by swallowing cyanide near Valmy, France.

Hitler appointed Field Marshal Walther Model as the new German commander in France. Sometimes known as "Hitler's fireman," he was highly respected for his defensive success on the Russian front. For almost three years Model had slowed the Red

Army's advance, and had done a masterful job restoring German battle lines after the Russian Operation Bagration offensive in early 1944. Model was the youngest field marshal in the German army, and a devoted follower of the Führer.

In Paris the situation was also highly precarious. The overall occupation commander in France, General Karl Heinrich von Stülpnagel, who was heavily implicated in the July 20 plot, had been relieved, and after a failed suicide attempt was awaiting trial in Berlin. The Paris occupation commander, General Hans von Boineburg-Lengsfeld, was peripherally implicated in the July 20 plot and was relieved of command on August 3.* To fill the vacancy, Hitler chose General Dietrich von Choltitz, who was then commanding a corps on the Western Front. Von Choltitz was recommended to Hitler by General Wilhelm Burgdorff, the chief of army personnel at Hitler's headquarters in East Prussia, because von Choltitz's loyalty to Hitler and the Third Reich had never flagged. After the July 20 plot, Hitler needed commanders who were loyal, and both Model and von Choltitz fit the bill. Von Choltitz was also a commander who, in Burgdorff's words, "never questioned an order no matter how harsh it was."[1] If Paris was to be defended to the end, von Choltitz was the man to do so.

Because of the importance Hitler attached to defending Paris, he wanted to meet von Choltitz personally. On Hitler's orders,

---

* General von Boineburg-Lengsfeld was a highly decorated war hero who had been badly injured when accidentally run over by a German tank during the Battle of Stalingrad in December 1942. After many months in the hospital he returned to active duty in July 1943 as commandant of Paris. His involvement in the July 20 plot came only after Hitler was reported dead, when, pursuant to General von Stülpnagel's orders, he supervised the arrest of the one thousand two hundred SS and Gestapo members in Paris. He was never prosecuted and finished the war as the commander of Maneuver Area Bergen.

Field Marshal Walther Model (left)

von Choltitz came by train to the Wolf's Lair, the Führer's head-quarters in Rastenburg, East Prussia, on August 6. Von Choltitz's military record was exemplary. In May 1940, as a lieutenant colonel, he had led the German paratroop attack on Rotterdam. After the bombardment of Rotterdam, during a meeting with the Dutch discussing the terms of surrender, the popular German general Kurt Student was shot in the head. Von Choltitz intervened and prevented the execution of all the Dutch who were present at the meeting. In July 1942 he led the attack on the Russian fortress of Sebastopol and was promoted to general after capturing it. His regiment began its assault with 4,800 men. When it was over, only 349 survived, and von Choltitz had been wounded in the arm. In 1943, he assisted in the German retreat in Russia, faithfully executing all of the orders he was given. That ensured his reputation as a general who never questioned an order.* He was sent to Italy in early 1944, where he commanded an armored corps attempting to smash the Anzio beachhead, and then was given command of the Eighty-Fourth Korps facing the Americans in Normandy.

Von Choltitz went to Hitler's headquarters with confidence. He believed that Germany could still win the war and, as he expressed it in his memoirs, was anxious "to be convinced again by Hitler" that that was the case. He wanted, above all, to leave the meeting "with his spirit raised by Hitler, reassured that there was still a chance to change the course of the war."[2] When he arrived he was met by General Burgdorff. Why, he asked Burgdorff, had he been chosen for the Paris assignment? "Because we know you can do the job that has to be done there," Burgdorff replied.[3]

But the meeting with Hitler turned into a disaster. As soon as he saw the Führer, von Choltitz realized the war was lost. Hitler was not the same man he had met in 1943 at Field Marshal Erich von Manstein's headquarters on the Russian front, where von Choltitz had sat opposite the Führer at a lunch given by Manstein. Von Choltitz was shocked at how Hitler looked. "I saw an old, bent-over, flabby man with thinning grey hair—a trembling, physically demolished human being. I had been told not to press his hand too hard since it had been injured in the plot. When I placed my right hand carefully into his, he gave me a grateful glance, the only one in a horrible hour."[4]

Hitler began the meeting by talking in a quiet tone about his

---

* British Intelligence secretly recorded the conversations of captured German generals while they were incarcerated at a prison camp in Great Britain. On August 29, 1944, von Choltitz was recorded saying the following to General Wilhelm von Thoma: "The worst job I ever carried out—which however I carried out with great consistency—was the liquidation of the Jews. I carried out this order down to the very last detail." *Taping Hitler's Generals: Transcripts of Secret Conversations, 1942–45*, Sönke Neitzel, ed. (St. Paul, MN: Frontline Books, 2007), 192.

General Dietrich von Choltitz

early career, how he founded the Nazi Party and molded it to govern Germany. No nation in the world will be able to defeat a people that has such a party organization, said Hitler. "The more he talked about events of the past, the more his voice rose uncontrollably. Finally, he spoke of the war and recent events."

He began with Normandy and the invasion and the German soldiers fighting there. I used a pause in his speech to say: "My Führer, I am the commander of the 84th Korps in Normandy and have come to . . ." He interrupted me immediately, raising his hands and replying, "I am well informed," and continued with his harangue, saying he had hope that the counteroffensive would be successful and that the

enemy would be driven into the sea. Whether he was trying
to convince himself or whether he was saying this in order
to keep the people around him fighting was never clear to
me. Having just been in Normandy fighting for seven weeks
under constant bombardment and lacking the necessary
supplies, I knew the desperate face of the German soldier
who began to lose his will to fight.[5]

Hitler then ranted at the top of his voice about the July 20 plot.
As von Choltitz recalled,

I witnessed the terrible eruption of a hateful mind. He yelled
at me saying he was glad to have caught the entire opposition
in one stroke and that he would annihilate them. He spoke
in a bloodthirsty language with froth literally coming out of

Hitler after the July 20 plot, 1944

his mouth. His entire body trembled. Sweat was running down his face while he spoke excitedly about the hanging of the generals. I saw in front of me someone who had lost his mind. The entire tragedy of my country was made clear to me. The fact that the life of our nation was in the hands of an insane being who could no longer judge the situation or was unwilling to see it realistically depressed me immensely.[6]

Finally, Hitler ended his tirade and sank into his chair. After a considerable pause, he turned to the issue that had brought von Choltitz to his headquarters.

"You are going to Paris," said the Führer. At the present time, Hitler told him, the garrison in Paris was a disgrace. "The only fighting going on is over seats at the officers' mess." Von Choltitz's job, he said, was to make Paris "a frontline city" and restore "discipline among troops accustomed to easy living." Hitler said he was making von Choltitz a *Befehlshaber*, a fortress commander, and that Paris was to be considered a fortress under his command. "You will stamp out without pity any uprising by the civilian population, any act of terrorism, any act of sabotage against the German garrison. For that, Herr General, you will receive from me all the support you need."[7]

The interview was over. That evening, August 7, von Choltitz boarded the train for his return to Berlin. As he acknowledged later, "a heavy gloom" had settled over him. He had come to Rastenburg looking for encouragement. He was leaving shaken and demoralized. He now recognized that Germany would lose the war, and that Hitler was out of control. "I asked myself the difficult question of whether a general, a leader of men, can in his soul and in his conscience take the responsibility of sacrificing his poor soldiers for a cause that has lost all hope."[8] It was clear to von Choltitz as he left East Prussia that both Hitler and his staff had no idea how the war in France was going.

The train ride back was equally upsetting. Also on the train was Robert Ley, an SS *Reichsleiter* and head of the Nazi labor movement (DAF). Over a bottle of wine that evening, Ley told von Choltitz of a new law that Hitler had just approved called the *Sippenhaft* (imprisoned families). Under its terms, a general's family would be held responsible for his failings. In effect, they would become hostages, the guarantors of a general's conduct. And according to Ley, the law was very strict. If a general escaped German justice by being taken prisoner, his family could be executed. Von Choltitz was stunned. "For the first time in my life I heard the term '*Sippenhaft.*' My heart stopped and I was deeply ashamed that our country had fallen into that kind of behavior." Germany was returning to the Middle Ages, he told Ley.

"Yes, perhaps," Ley replied. "These are exceptional times." [9]

According to von Choltitz, Ley's answers were always "ice cold. He obviously lived in a different world than I did. I parted from him that evening deeply concerned about the fate of our nation and did not sleep that night." [10]

When von Choltitz arrived in Berlin the next morning, he was told that Hitler had promoted him to *general der infanterie*, the German equivalent of lieutenant general. On his way back to Paris, von Choltitz stopped briefly in Baden-Baden, where his family lived. His wife, Uberta, was the daughter of a general in Kaiser Wilhelm II's World War I army, and they had two daughters, age ten and eight, and a young son of four months. Von Choltitz himself descended from Prussian military aristocracy, and as a youth had served as a page in the court of the Queen of Saxony. He spent the morning of August 9 with his family—a painful reminder of the *Sippenhaft*—and then left for Paris by automobile, planning to arrive there before nightfall.

Von Choltitz was eager to return to Paris because General von Boineburg-Lengsfeld, the outgoing commander, had invited him to dinner that evening. The commander of the Paris occupation lived in an elegant townhouse at 26 Raspail, just across the Seine from the Louvre and the Tuileries. As soon as he saw it, von Choltitz told Boineburg-Lengsfeld that he didn't need the house. "For the days ahead, I need a headquarters, not a residence," said von Choltitz.[11] And he took rooms at the Hotel Meurice, where German headquarters was located.

The dinner that evening was an opportunity for von Choltitz to meet the senior officers of the command whom Boineburg-Lengsfeld had invited, and take their measure. The conversation was formal, and von Choltitz gave no indication of his change of heart. After dinner, von Choltitz and Boineburg-Lengsfeld, joined by Boineburg-Lengsfeld's chief of staff, Colonel Karl von Unger,

Hotel Meurice, Rue de Rivoli

and his aide, Dankwart von Arnim, had a long conversation over brandy and cigars. With the guests gone, the conversation took on an air of cold realism verging on outright resistance to Hitler's orders to destroy Paris. Boineburg-Lengsfeld and Unger appealed to von Choltitz to save the city. According to Arnim, "It was clear that Boineburg and Unger were on the best of terms with von Choltitz. . . . There was clearly an agreement to focus exclusively on military and administrative matters, and that the most important issue at stake was the future of Paris."[12] All three men agreed there was no military value in defending Paris, and that the city should be preserved. Arnim's notes of the meeting that evening are instructive in that they show that von Choltitz had already decided to save Paris rather than destroy it in battle.

Afterward, von Choltitz was driven back to the Hotel Meurice by Arnim. On the ride, Arnim asked him if he could be transferred to the Lehr Panzer Division in Normandy. Von Choltitz said no. He told Arnim that he had already talked to Boineburg-Lengsfeld about Arnim's future employment. He said he needed an aide whom he could trust, one who understood the complexities of Paris. He therefore needed Arnim to stay on, and Boineburg-Lengsfeld had agreed. Interestingly, von Choltitz and Arnim were distant relatives. Also, the fact that von Choltitz consulted Boineburg-Lengsfeld—who had been implicated in the July 20 plot—further suggests that von Choltitz did not become convinced to save Paris because of his exposure to the city. He had been determined to save it prior to his arrival. "I cannot implement this insane order," Arnim quotes von Choltitz as saying.[13]

The *Sippenhaft* was a major obstacle. If von Choltitz made it clear he was going to save Paris, his family in Baden-Baden might be executed. That concern motivated him throughout and helps explain why he would cover his tracks as best he could. And defense of the city was not easy. Hitler had told von Choltitz that he could keep all of the troops presently in Paris and place them under his command. That turned out not to be the case. Field Marshal Hugo Sparrle, chief of the Luftwaffe in France, and General Karl Kitzinger, who had succeeded Stülpnagel as overall occupation commander, had between them some six thousand men in Paris. They were immediately withdrawn.

That left von Choltitz with between twenty thousand and twenty-five thousand troops. Of those, two divisions, the Forty-Eighth and the 338th Infantry, were stationed across the Seine to guard approaches to the city. The remainder, some fifteen thousand men, remained in Paris. But for the most part they were not combat troops but members of the Paris garrison. Von Choltitz had little artillery and very few tanks. The available artillery were largely anti-aircraft guns manned by seventeen-year-olds who had never seen combat. And there were few experienced battlefield commanders. After quickly reviewing the situation, von Choltitz told General Günther Blumentritt, the operations officer at Kluge's headquarters, that they were facing a catastrophe of unimaginable dimensions. "No way," Blumentritt replied. "Don't speak about it." [14]

According to von Choltitz, original German plans called for suppressing revolt inside Paris but made no provision for defending the city from an Allied onslaught. "According to the original plan I was to have 36 different defensive positions in case there was a revolt inside the city. Was I to move all troops into the center of Paris and occupy major street intersections and the parks? This would not change the military situation. . . . And so I decided to keep order in the city with a minimum force and prepare for a defense—if you could call it that—outside the city." [15]

On August 10, von Choltitz's first full day in Paris, he met with the German ambassador to France, Otto Abetz. "We had a calm and leisurely talk," said von Choltitz. "I informed him of my role in Paris and mentioned the threat we faced. Abetz listened calmly.

After a conversation that lasted forty-five minutes, I said to him, 'Mr. Ambassador, we live here together and must stay in contact.' He then thanked me for my unvarnished presentation of the situation. I could not tell whether he was surprised or whether he had expected it." [16]

To clarify the command structure, on Sunday, August 13, von Choltitz drove himself to see Field Marshal von Kluge at his headquarters in Saint-Germain-en-Laye. Von Choltitz wanted command of all the troops in the area, not just in Paris itself, and he also sought reinforcements. Kluge agreed on both points, but the reinforcements would have to wait. In Kluge's view, they were not yet required. As for the command structure, Kluge asked von Choltitz when he departed, "Are you now satisfied?"

"Field Marshal, until now it was a military funeral without honors. It now may be one with military honors." [17]

Two days later Kluge convened a meeting of military commanders at his headquarters to transmit the Führer's order for a scorched-earth policy in Paris. The plan was presented by General Blumentritt, who said it was "strategically essential." If Paris's industry was not crippled, it could be turned against Germany in a matter of weeks. That included the city's gas, electricity, and water systems. On the other hand, "setting the population into turmoil and paralyzing the city" would slow the Allied advance. Von Choltitz was not surprised. Blumentritt was simply putting Hitler's orders into effect. But von Choltitz objected to the timing. He told the meeting he was interested in defending Paris, not destroying it. The time to put Blumentritt's program into effect was when they were abandoning the city. Launching the program prematurely would throw thousands of factory workers into the hands of the Resistance. And besides, "German soldiers drink water, too." [18]

Von Choltitz carried the day. But the victory was brief. Just before he was relieved by Hitler, Kluge ordered von Choltitz to commence the demolition of the bridges in Paris. "The situation had turned dramatic," said von Choltitz. The Allies were advancing. Von Choltitz said the information he had was that they would surround the city for safekeeping. "What value would the detonation have? I also needed the bridges myself to move troops within the city. And finally, what a barbaric order I was asked to execute."[19]

Von Choltitz told higher headquarters that he could not blow up the bridges since he did not have the explosives or the men to implant them. At Hitler's headquarters in East Prussia, chief of operations Alfred Jodl responded by assigning a veteran engineer unit with explosives to do the job. The unit was commanded by Captain Werner Ebernach, an old friend of von Choltitz from before the war. In 1936 at army maneuvers in Gimna, Saxony, Ebernach had blown up two bridges across the Mulde River, which von Choltitz had seen. Now he had been ordered to destroy all sixty-five of Paris's bridges. "Go ahead into the preparations," von Choltitz told him. "But do not detonate anything without my personal approval. The Seine is not the Mulde and Paris is not Gimna. We have the whole world watching us here, not just a handful of generals."[20]

As von Choltitz expressed it,

It was my responsibility to maintain order with the available troops and to facilitate the withdrawal of troops passing through the city. Whether blowing up the bridges was part of this responsibility was entirely my decision. It made my situation more difficult. Beyond my military consideration it was my firm intent to protect the civilian population and their beautiful city. Both motives, different in their intent, were part of my concept of being a soldier. They pointed in the same direction: I had to do everything possible to avoid the destruction of Paris.[21]

On August 16, von Choltitz was called on by Paris officials in his office at the Meurice. The officials were concerned about the explosives that had been planted not only in the bridges, but also in the walls of power plants, telephone exchanges, electricity works, and gas installations. It was obvious that they would be set off when the Germans withdrew. They appealed to von Choltitz to spare the facilities.

"I allowed these gentlemen to speak and was deeply impressed by their civility, intelligence, and courage," said von Choltitz. "In the end, I rose from my seat and told them that fate had made us neighbors and that we would stay that way. The war had brought an endless tragedy and that I had no desire to burden our nations with more of it. I would order that the installations they were concerned about not be destroyed."[22]

There was one condition. French officials should maintain order in the city, said von Choltitz, and he would remove the explosives. And he did. At von Choltitz's order, explosives were removed from the power plants, gas installations, and telephone exchanges. Afterward the French commented on von Choltitz's moderation and the total absence of the brutality his predecessors had shown.[23]

Von Choltitz was surprised on August 17 when Field Marshal Walther Model suddenly appeared in his office. Model and von Choltitz knew each other from the Russian front, and Model had just arrived after a thirty-six-hour trip. Model told von Choltitz that he had come to replace Kluge, who had just been relieved. Von Choltitz asked Model whether Kluge had known about the July 20 plot. Model nodded. "In this moment I realized the depth of the tragedy playing out here. Field Marshal von Kluge was on his way to the gallows."

"I studied Model's face intently," said von Choltitz.

I believe that he knew he was faced with a painful task. The Field Marshal was a brave and determined soldier; a man who often with his small plane landed in the middle of fighting troops in order to give the necessary instructions. Now he had been named the commander of the army group and the Normandy front. I told him about the situation in Paris and what I was doing. He appeared to agree. At least he did not say anything to the contrary. I did not mention the order to blow up the bridges. The often injured general appeared so tired after his trip, I didn't feel I should discuss difficult questions with him. After a frugal lunch, he departed for his headquarters. I never saw him again.[24]

Model would kill himself in Germany in April 1945.

Von Choltitz also intervened to prevent the execution of thousands of prisoners held by the SS and Gestapo in concentration camps and prisons around the city. Two days after ordering the explosives removed, he was called on by the Swedish consul general in Paris, Raoul Nordling, who raised the question of the po-

Raoul Nordling

litical prisoners held in the city. He told von Choltitz he was afraid the SS would use the German pullout from the city as an excuse to execute the prisoners. Von Choltitz later described Nordling as "a brave representative of humanity."[25]

As they were discussing the issue, General Carl Oberg, head of the SS in France, arrived and said he had been ordered to evacuate the prisons and camps. After he departed, von Choltitz asked Nordling for his opinion. Nordling said he thought it was of "the utmost importance to prevent the massacre of the prisoners."[26] Von Choltitz agreed but said the prisoners were not his responsibility and he could not discharge them. They belonged to the military commander in France, whose office was in the Majestic Hotel. He gave Nordling a letter urging the prisoners' release and told him to take it to a Major Huhm at the Majestic. "But you had better hurry," von Choltitz told him. "Major Huhm leaves Paris at noon."[27]

At the Majestic, Huhm met Nordling immediately and, after looking at von Choltitz's letter, agreed to cooperate. A contract was drawn up providing for the transfer of the prisoners, camps, and hospitals to Nordling assisted by the Red Cross.[28] In return, five German POWs would be released for every prisoner let go, but as Huhm said, "it's only a formality." Nordling returned the contract to von Choltitz, who immediately signed it. More than three thousand prisoners were quickly released into Nordling's custody from five prisons, three camps, and three hospitals. At one camp, the SS commander refused to comply, and von Choltitz sent his ranking staff officer, Colonel Heigen, to enforce the order. At another, 850 prisoners had already been loaded on a train, but a German general at a suburban station who received a copy of the contract ordered the prisoners' release. When Heinrich Himmler heard about the arrangement, he did his best to overrule von Choltitz, but by then it was too late. With the Gestapo in retreat, there was nothing he could do.

Von Choltitz also did his best to keep Paris supplied. As he expressed it, "Paris had no coal, the Metro had stopped running, and electricity was only available for a few hours each day. I worried much about providing for the four-and-a-half million inhabitants. . . . I decided to feed the population using the army's provisions. But this proved difficult. While some parts of the city were completely quiet, other parts were upset in anger. I could understand all this, but it certainly made the distribution of food more difficult."[29]

As the Allies approached, the Resistance in Paris became bolder. On August 19, three thousand members of the Paris police switched sides and took control of the *préfecture* (police headquarters) and adjoining buildings near Notre-Dame. Von Choltitz responded carefully. He dispatched a few troops and a few tanks to isolate the *préfecture*, but declined to storm the building—which he easily could have done. Instead, he discussed the situation with Nordling, who had come to his office. "I released prisoners, and what happened? Terrorists took the Prefecture, and they are shooting just under my windows. . . . I have to maintain order, and I will maintain order. I will destroy the Prefecture." But then von Choltitz paused. "I was at Stalingrad. Since then I have done nothing but maneuver to avoid encirclement. Retreat after retreat, defeat after defeat. And here I am now in Paris. What will happen to this marvelous city?"[30]

Nordling responded quickly. "If you destroy the Prefecture, you will also destroy Notre Dame and the Sainte-Chapelle. And to what end?" Nordling urged von Choltitz to think about the future, about what future historians might write about the destruction of Paris.[31]

Von Choltitz was moved. "If there were only leaders among the insurgents, we could find a *modus vivendi*, but with whom am I supposed to negotiate?"[32] Nordling once again sprang into action.

Shortly after eight that evening he was in the *préfecture* laying out the terms of a truce. Von Choltitz, he told the leadership of the insurrection, was ready to recognize the combatants in the *préfecture de police* as the civil authority responsible for Paris, to treat those captured as prisoners of war, to respect all the local occupied administrations, and to aid in supplying food and water to Paris, all on the condition that the truce be respected.

For the Resistance, the offer was a godsend. They were virtually out of ammunition, and the Germans could storm the *préfecture* almost at will. At 9 p.m. on August 19, the leaders of the Resistance accepted von Choltitz's offer in principle. The truce had been agreed on. Working it out in practice would take effort, and it would never fully succeed. But for the moment peace had been restored in Paris, and the destruction of its historic buildings had been avoided.

That same day von Choltitz had been visited by three SS officers from Berlin. They had come to Paris on Hitler's orders, they told him, to remove the Bayeux Tapestry from the Louvre and take it to Berlin. The tapestry is an enormous embroidered cloth that depicts the Battle of Hastings. Von Choltitz had been told the night before by the local SS commander that the men would be coming, and had agreed with the German army's art curator in Paris that they would lose the keys to the Louvre. But that was not necessary. Much of the Louvre was now under the control of the Resistance. Von Choltitz told the visitors it would not be a problem. He could provide them with weapons and they could force their way in. "Surely, you'll manage to fetch the tapestry from the cellar, it's a trifling job . . . for the Führer's best soldiers." [33] The SS men were startled. They had not expected to have to fight for the tapestry, and were unprepared. After brief reflection they told von Choltitz they didn't believe the tapestry was in the Louvre and returned to Berlin.

German troops in Paris, August 1944

The truce Nordling had negotiated was not totally successful. Communist resistance fighters refused to accept it, and so did the SS. But those were exceptions. For the most part the truce held. Under its terms, German battle troops moving eastward through Paris would use the outer boulevards and avoid the center of the city. The Resistance (FFI) members were recognized as soldiers and treated according to the laws of war. At 2 p.m. on August 20, the Resistance began the circulation throughout Paris of the following notice:

> In light of the German High Command's agreement to refrain from attacking public buildings occupied by French troops and to treat French prisoners in accordance with the laws of war, the Provisional Government of the French Republic and the National Committee of Liberation ask you to cease firing on the occupiers until Paris has been completely

evacuated. The greatest calm is recommended and the population is urged to avoid the streets.[34]

Von Choltitz did not want the truce announced over the radio because he believed it would get back to Hitler's headquarters. Instead, German military vehicles and French police cars drove through the city with loudspeakers announcing it. The Paris *préfecture de police*, speaking for the Provisional Government of the French Republic, also ordered a suspension of arms. Parisians were overwhelmingly delighted and welcomed the truce warmly. French flags were displayed throughout the city, there was dancing in the streets, and stores and cafés remained open.

On August 20, Hitler issued an order to Field Marshal Model that German forces were to hold fast at the Seine and that Paris was to become the *Schwerpunkt* (strong point) of the defense line. "The Paris bridgehead is to be held at all costs, if necessary without regard to the destruction of the city."[35] Model had been in command only three days, but he realized that Hitler's order would mean the final defeat of the German army in France and would open the door for the Allies to advance into Germany. He replied that he could hold Paris with two hundred thousand more troops and six additional Panzer divisions. But without them he was withdrawing behind the city and would try to form a battle line on the Marne and the Somme. "Tell the Führer that I know what I am doing," he told an incredulous General Alfred Jodl, at Hitler's headquarters.[36] On August 20, Model ordered the German First Army and Fifth Panzer Army to evacuate their positions in front of Paris, cross the Seine over the bridges that still existed in the city, and move north. The defense of Paris would be left to von Choltitz.

But the peace in Paris was shaky. It was aided slightly on the 21st when German soldiers captured three of the leaders of the

Resistance, including Alexandre Parodi, de Gaulle's minister in Paris. The three were brought to von Choltitz's office in the Hotel Meurice, and von Choltitz impressed on them the importance of maintaining the truce. If fighting broke out again, the consequences would be tragic, he said.

Parodi replied that he too wanted peace and order in the city. But he said, "You, General, command an army. You give orders and your men obey. The Resistance is made up of many movements, and I do not control them all." [37] Von Choltitz understood, but hoped something could come from the meeting. He ordered the three men released to Nordling's custody, and they luckily avoided being killed by the SS, which was waiting for them on the street outside von Choltitz's office.

Von Choltitz recognized that his days in Paris were numbered. Model had withdrawn the forces in front of the city, and the Resistance was growing bolder. On the night of August 21 von Choltitz wrote to his wife, Uberta, in Baden-Baden: "Our task is hard and our days grow difficult. I try always to do my duty, and must often ask God to help me find the paths on which it lies." He asked Uberta if their four-month-old son, Timo, had started to cut his teeth, and told her to kiss their daughters for him. "They must be proud of their father, no matter what the future holds." [38] Von Choltitz gave the letter to his cousin Adolf von Carlowitz, who was leaving Paris to return to Germany.

The next day von Choltitz met again with Nordling, over drinks in von Choltitz's office. "Don't tell the English, but I'm going to have a whisky," said von Choltitz. After swallowing the whisky in one gulp, von Choltitz began the conversation. "Your truce, Herr Counsel General, doesn't seem to be working very well." Von Choltitz said the three prisoners he had released had done nothing to improve the truce, and the insurrection was growing.

Nordling was briefly taken aback. There was only one person the Resistance really obeyed and that was General de Gaulle, he said. But de Gaulle was not in Paris. He was probably with the Allies in Normandy.

"Why doesn't someone go to see him?" asked von Choltitz.

Nordling was struck by von Choltitz's directness. Would he authorize someone to pass through German lines to see the Allies?

"Why not?" von Choltitz replied.

Nordling responded as von Choltitz hoped he would. As a diplomat, he was prepared to take on the mission to the Allies if he had a valid pass.

Von Choltitz nodded. He then laid on his desk the orders he had received both from Berlin and from Model to begin the destruction of Paris. He told Nordling that despite the orders he had tried to effect a truce, but it was becoming increasingly obvious that the truce had failed. Very soon, he said, he was going to have to carry out the orders he had been given or he would be relieved. The only thing that would prevent that would be rapid arrival of the Allies in Paris.

"You must realize that my behavior in telling you this could be interpreted as treason, because what I am really doing is asking the Allies to help me."

Nordling was overwhelmed by what von Choltitz was saying. And he realized that his own words to the Allies might not be enough to convince them of what von Choltitz had just said. So he asked von Choltitz for a document he could give the Allies.

Von Choltitz declined. "I could not possibly put what I have just said on paper." But he then wrote out in longhand a statement that would permit Nordling to pass through German lines: "The Commanding General of Greater Paris authorizes the Consul General of Sweden R. Nordling to leave Paris and its line of defense." He also said that if Nordling had difficulty getting through

German lines to call him and he would repeat the instructions over the telephone.

Nordling agreed to try. Von Choltitz was visibly relieved. He had found a way to warn the Allies of the danger hanging over Paris, and tell them that the road to the city was open. How long it would remain open was impossible to tell, and if the Allies didn't come soon, he would have to take the action ordered and destroy the city.

"Go fast," he told Nordling. "Twenty-four, forty-eight hours are all you have. After that, I cannot promise you what will happen here."[39]

— V —

The Resistance Rises

"From a military point of view, I was not too concerned about the Resistance. But psychologically it was a highly dangerous situation."

—GENERAL DIETRICH VON CHOLTITZ

The Paris Resistance began slowly. And like all resistance movements, it brought together a motley collection of patriots. The Allies assisted it only sparingly, and de Gaulle did his best to control it, but that was always a challenge. The leader of the Paris Resistance was Henri Tanguy, better known as Colonel Rol. The thirty-eight-year-old Rol was by trade a sheet metal worker, labor organizer, and dedicated Communist. He was a veteran of the International Brigade, which had fought against Franco in the Spanish Civil War, and afterward served as an antitank gunner in the French Army in 1940, earning the *Croix de Guerre* for his service.

In October 1940, Rol began to organize small resistance cells in French labor unions, and in 1942 was one of the founding members of the *Francs-Tireurs et Partisans*—an anti-German resistance group taking the name of fighters against the Prussians in 1870–71. The *Francs-Tireurs* became one of the most active resistance groups in Paris, concentrating on preventing the arrests and deportation of political prisoners. In September 1943, the French

Colonel Rol

Forces of the Interior (FFI) selected Rol to command operations in Paris, and on June 5, 1944—the day before the landing of Allied troops in Normandy—he was given command of all FFI forces in the *Île-de-France*, an area encompassing not only Paris and its suburbs, but the four surrounding departments as well. Technically Rol was under General Koenig and de Gaulle. But as a practical matter he was his own boss.

One of the major problems confronting the FFI was a shortage of combatants and weapons. Rol could initially count on only 155 men in Paris who were trained and fully armed.[1] Most others were untrained civilians armed with obsolete weapons, and there was precious little ammunition. Rol repeatedly asked the Allies to supply weapons, but found little interest among Allied leaders. He responded by attempting to seize German weapons, but again with little success. In mid-July, the seven hundred FFI members in Paris's 7th Arrondissement had just three submachine guns, twenty rifles, and a few pistols.[2]

From D-Day on, Rol was determined to launch an insurrection in Paris. He reacted negatively to General Koenig's order of June 10 to stop guerrilla activity because of the slow progress of Allied forces in Normandy, and was convinced that once the insurrection started it would be impossible to put down. Both de Gaulle and Koenig considered the FFI as part of the Free French army and looked on an uprising in Paris as a military issue. Rol by contrast saw it as a political and moral issue. He firmly believed that it was important for Parisians to liberate their city, thereby earning the right to govern themselves. Rol was a Communist politically, but partisan ideology was not his principal motivation. He wanted Paris to be able to stand on its own feet and avoid Allied control.

De Gaulle sought to manage Rol and the FFI by dispatching Jacques Delmas (codename Chaban) to Paris as his military rep-

Chaban-Delmas

resentative. A handsome and charismatic former rugby player, Chaban—at the age of twenty-nine—was the youngest general in the French army and a devoted admirer of de Gaulle. His mission was to sneak into Paris and bring order and discipline to the FFI. Above all, he was to delay an FFI insurrection until the Allies approached. He was partially successful. Rol reluctantly agreed to obey Koenig's order of June 10 to delay guerrilla actions, but held to his view that a revolt should begin before an Allied move on Paris, in order to demonstrate the power of the French people to liberate themselves. He also believed the FFI should rise up on its own to show that it was independent of the Allied armies.

Alexandre Parodi was de Gaulle's political representative in Paris. Parodi held the position of *délégué generale* (delegate general) for the Provisional Government of the French Republic. His assignment was to bring the authority of the Provisional Government to Paris. Like Chaban-Delmas, Parodi was directed to prevent a premature insurrection in Paris, and above all to ensure that a liberated Paris was ruled by the Provisional Government, not the Communists or the supporters of Marshal Pétain. Memories of past revolutions—above all, the Paris Commune of 1871— hung over the city, and Parodi was to ensure that such a tragedy did not happen again. As de Gaulle instructed him, "Always speak out loudly and clearly in the name of the State."[3]

With the Allies bogged down in Normandy, Rol found himself with little alternative but to order the FFI to stand down and wait. He urged Chaban-Delmas to try to arrange more arms drops, but understood when Chaban-Delmas said it was de Gaulle he worked for. And the military situation did not look good in June. Not only were Allied troops still in their original beachheads, but the Germans had begun their V-1 rocket attacks against targets in Great Britain. In June 1944, the Germans launched 2,452 V-1 rockets, approximately 800 of which fell on London. German

Alexandre Parodi

propaganda boasted that the rockets would end the war and bring Britain to its knees. They also promised even greater destruction when the technically more sophisticated V-2 and V-3 rockets were launched. Not so curiously, Parisians seemed to ignore the German rocket attacks. Many if not most Parisians disliked the British, and were little concerned about the damage inflicted.

The stalemate in Normandy led many Parisians to turn to the Russian front, where the Red Army was moving ahead quickly. This was particularly true of the Communist Party (PCF), which delighted in reminding Parisians of the Franco-Russian alliance before World War I. As Bastille Day (July 14) approached, the leaders of the Communist Party decided to break with the underground French leadership and urge a major uprising. Celebrations of Bastille Day had been banned by the Vichy government, and this would be the first since 1939. Chaban and Parodi were against the idea, pointing out that an insurrection in Paris was premature and would undoubtedly fail. Rol too was against it, noting that the Allies were still bogged down. Accordingly, he told the FFI to remain underground. Rol was not against a Paris uprising, but July 14 was too early.

The Communists went ahead with the labor strikes they had planned for Bastille Day. The strikes took place in the working-class districts of eastern Paris, and involved at least 100,000 workers. But most of Paris was not affected. A more significant development was that the Paris police were conspicuous by their inactivity. Demonstrations throughout the city on Bastille Day were not interrupted, and the police watched with tacit support. For Rol and other leaders of the FFI the message was clear. The tide in the city was clearly turning in favor of the Resistance. The police were on their side.

After the demonstrations of July 14, Rol had begun to develop new plans for a revolt whenever an opportunity presented itself. The main problem was the continuing lack of arms. Rol stepped up his pleas to London for more weapons, but with no success. The Paris Resistance leadership began to suspect that the refusal of the Allies to provide weapons was part of a larger plan to impose American military government on France. In reality, the Allies did not see how they could air-drop weapons into Paris without their falling into the hands of the Germans. Another fear was that to arm the Paris Resistance would be to arm the Communists, who might use the weapons to seize control. But the message was clear. If the FFI was going to take on the Germans in Paris, they would have to do so without Allied help.[4]

The attempted assassination of Hitler on July 20, followed by the breakthrough in Normandy by General J. Lawton Collins's VII

Corps on July 26, added to the change of mood in Paris. As Patton's Third Army raced eastward, the FFI stepped up its planning for action. The downside was that the FFI was led by Communists, and the possibility that the Communists might seize control of Paris became a major concern. As de Gaulle wrote, "If the Communists establish a base of power in Paris, they will have an easy time establishing a government. . . . They can present themselves as the leaders of an insurrection and a kind of commune. That such an insurrection in the capital would, for certain, lead to a power dominated by the Third International I have known for a long time."[5] The specter of the Paris Commune of 1871 continued to haunt de Gaulle's Provisional Government. Chaban-Delmas and Parodi did their utmost to contain that possibility, but it lurked in the background. The best way to prevent it would be for the Allied armies to arrive as soon as possible.

Then suddenly Warsaw erupted. On August 1, as the Red Army approached the city, the Home Army made up of Polish resisters led an uprising against the German occupiers. The Home Army believed that with the Soviets approaching, the Germans would leave quickly. But the Red Army, reluctant to help the anti-Communist leadership of the Home Army, halted outside Warsaw. And the Germans, led by the SS, wreaked vengeance on the city. Reichsführer Heinrich Himmler gave orders to destroy the city and kill the inhabitants. In the end, one-quarter of the buildings in Warsaw were destroyed and an estimated 200,000 Poles were killed. The Red Army stood by and allowed the Germans to slaughter the USSR's political opponents.[6]

The fear of another self-destructive Warsaw Uprising helped keep Paris quiet as the Allies advanced. Schools remained open, many Parisians sunbathed along the Seine, and the racing season continued at Longchamps and Auteuil. Cinemas showed films with projectors using electricity generated by teams of bicycles,

Edith Piaf and Yves Montand sang at the Moulin Rouge, and more than twenty theaters produced plays for packed houses. Unlike Warsaw, or London or Berlin for that matter, Paris remained intact. And de Gaulle's representatives, Chaban-Delmas and Parodi, were determined to keep it so.

To forestall a premature insurrection, in early August Chaban-Delmas was able surreptitiously to fly to London, where he urged Allied officials to come quickly. But the effort was useless. Everyone who saw Chaban-Delmas, including General Sir Hastings Ismay, Churchill's military aide, said the same: there would be no change in Allied plans simply to remedy Paris's political problems. But Chaban-Delmas had at least made the Allies aware of the problem, and that was important. In the days ahead, Allied awareness, particularly among the Free French leadership, would be important in providing Eisenhower with a reason to change plans.

And the Allies continued to refuse to supply the Paris Resistance with weapons. When General Koenig asked the Allies to drop forty thousand Sten guns to assist the Resistance in the Paris region, the British objected. "There will always be the temptation to put them to mischievous uses should political passions be inflamed when the war is over," said the Foreign Office.[7]

As August wore on, the mood in Paris became more militant. Parodi increasingly came to believe that Rol and the *Comité Parisien de la Libération* (CPL) were fully qualified to lead the Resistance and should be accepted. "You must give us your confidence and your support in this affair so we can come to an agreement and the Government's authority maintained," he told the Provisional Government in Algiers. Receiving no reply, two days later Parodi met with the CPL and came to an agreement recognizing that the CPL "alone has the authority to lead the national insurrection in the region and receive the Allies in Paris." Again, no reply from Algiers.

Rol followed through on August 7, issuing an alert to all FFI forces in the Paris region:

> The main characteristic of the Allied offensive is that the Wehrmacht is completely unable to resist in the current theatre of operations. In the Paris region, there is nothing to indicate that the enemy has decided to carry out a determined resistance. . . . The Allied offensive, the precarious situation of the Wehrmacht and the recent events of 14 July 1944 all indicate that we are on the eve of an insurrection in our region.[8]

At the same time, conditions in Paris were rapidly eroding. Food was now in short supply. Dr. Jean-Marie Musy, the senior Red Cross representative in Paris, published a report at the beginning of August describing the problem. Bread supplies were 60 percent of what they had been five years earlier; milk was down to 12 percent, meat was at 20 percent, and vegetable supplies had dropped to 10 percent. "The capital is threatened with famine," said Dr. Musy.[9]

On August 12, Paris railway workers went on strike. This action was not coordinated with the Resistance, but called by the French railway workers' union (CGT), which had been banned under Vichy. The strike was not totally effective, some workers refusing to walk out, and the German military did what it could to keep trains moving. But the strike had an effect. It was the beginning of the revolt.

The next action came two days later when Resistance groups in the Paris police met to devise strategy. The police enjoyed a mixed reputation. In 1940 they had done nothing to challenge the German occupation, and in the following three years had performed some of the most despicable tasks of the Vichy government, including the roundup and deportation of Paris's Jewish population. But gradually, as Allied victory became evident, many of the police inwardly changed sides. By 1944 there were three Resistance groups in the police department, comprising about 10 percent of the total force. The first group formed was the *Honneur de la Police*, a Gaullist organization that included some of the highest-ranking police officers. It contained about 400 members. The second was the *Police et Patrie*, a socialist organization containing some 250 officers and 400 non-uniformed police employees. This group was active in supplying identity cards to resisters and escaped prisoners. The largest group was the *Front National de la Police*, a Communist group, containing some 800 members and many more sympathizers in the police force. Directed by the French Communist Party (PCF), it was distrusted by the other two groups, who feared it might be the vanguard of a Communist coup. Thus far the three groups had worked independently, but as the crisis of liberation approached, it seemed time to bring them together.

On August 14, Rol and Parodi convened a meeting of all three groups. The Germans had begun to disarm the police in the Paris suburbs of St. Denis and Asnières, and it seemed a prelude to what might happen in Paris. Rol and the *Front National* argued that the Paris police should immediately go on strike to prevent themselves from being disarmed. It would also show the population of Paris that the police were on their side. The faults of the past three years would be forgiven, and the police might regain the respect they had lost. The *Front National* leaders argued that any policeman who did not go on strike should be considered a traitor.

The Gaullist *Honneur de la Police* argued against going on strike and suggested it would split the force at a time when unity was required. The socialist *Police et Patrie* also thought a strike was not only premature, but might lead Paris into becoming another Warsaw. Rol carried the day when he pointed out that if the *Front National* went on strike, it and the Communist Party would get the credit for the liberation while the other groups, and the police more generally, would be condemned for their continued association with the occupiers. After much discussion, the three groups agreed to strike and to distribute leaflets printed on both sides. On one side would be an appeal by the FFI for the Paris police to go on strike. On the other, a statement by the three Resistance groups to go on strike as well: "For the final combat, everyone must go forward with the people of Paris."[10] Their message was quickly distributed throughout the city:

> The hour of liberation has arrived. Today it is the duty of the police to join the FFI. You will do nothing further to help the enemy maintain order. You will refuse to arrest patriots, to check identities, to guard prisons, and so forth. You will aid the FFI in putting down anyone who continues to serve the enemy. Police who do not obey these orders will be considered traitors and collaborators. . . . On no pretext allow yourself to be disarmed. . . . March with the people of Paris to the final battle.[11]

The strike began the next morning, August 15. The streets of Paris were empty of police. Almost all members of the force obeyed the call to strike. Of the fifteen thousand police officers in Paris, not more than a hundred showed up for work. And the strikers kept their weapons. The FFI took advantage of the strike and began to move around the city wearing the armband of liberation—the Cross of Lorraine. As Raoul Nordling, the Swedish consul general, said, "The situation inside Paris was entirely transformed in the space of a few hours. We knew that somewhere in the shadows great events were transpiring that could perhaps unleash rivers of blood." [12]

August 15 also saw Allied forces land on France's Mediterranean coast (Operation Dragoon). With an invasion fleet of six hundred vessels, including six battleships and four aircraft carriers, American and Free French forces came ashore on a thirty-five-mile front just east of Toulon. By evening the beachhead was secure and the Allied troops were moving inland. The American Seventh Army, under Lieutenant General Alexander Patch, and the First French Army, under General Jean de Lattre de Tassigny, were heading north. In Paris, news of the landings spread quickly. The BBC announced the news shortly after the troops went ashore, and the cafés were buzzing. Celebrations were widespread. The port of Marseilles would soon be captured by the First French Army in undamaged condition, and Patch's Seventh Army was advancing up the *Route Napoléon* and would reach Grenoble on August 20. Even more important, Patton's Third Army was in Chartres, just ninety-five kilometers to the southwest of Paris. Liberation seemed imminent.

The combination of the police strike and the Allied advance quickly changed the mood in Paris. The Germans stood by and watched it happen. Von Choltitz believed it was better to have the police on strike, but still politically neutral, than push them into the Resistance. And without the police, the citizens of Paris became nervous. Was their absence the beginning of anarchy and revolution? Rol and the PCF hoped so. The Germans for their part hoped that the police were just balking at plans to disarm them— an order that could be rectified. Collaborationists were particularly worried because their protection was disappearing. And the police played their cards close to their chest. Although they refused to go to work, they also were careful not to engage in any anti-German activities so long as the Germans didn't try to disarm them.

The police strike motivated others. On August 16, workers for Paris's subway, the Métro, the telephone and telegraph company, and the railroad went on strike. These strikes hit the Germans more than the Parisians since the Métro and railroads were being used almost exclusively by the German occupying authority. But when postal workers went out on strike the next day, Parisians felt the impact. Meanwhile, Allied forces continued their advance. On August 19, Patton's forces reached the Seine, just thirty-five miles west of Paris. "I pissed in the Seine this morning," the general told Omar Bradley.[13]

De Gaulle and the Free French leadership were keenly aware of the need to control any Paris insurrection. In early August, de Gaulle had dispatched Charles Luizet to Paris to take control of the Paris police on behalf of the Provisional Government. Luizet had been a roommate of General Leclerc at the Saint-Cyr military academy, where he studied under de Gaulle. He had joined the Free French in July 1940 and had been the head of Free French intelligence operations in North Africa. When Corsica was liberated in 1943, Luizet was appointed the prefect. De Gaulle recognized the importance of being in control of the police before the Allies arrived in Paris. He gave Luizet a written order from the Provisional Government appointing him the prefect of police and told him to get to Paris as soon as possible. Luizet left Corsica on August 2, but after a tortuous trip did not arrive in Paris until the 17th, only to find that the police were on strike.

Luizet met immediately with Parodi and Chaban-Delmas, who were skeptical both of the strike and of a possible insurrection. Luizet disagreed. With Allied forces close by, he believed the strike by Paris police was the first step in the insurrection. If the Gaullists did not move quickly to gain control, then Rol and the FFI would. As Luizet saw it, he and Parodi and Chaban-Delmas had to move quickly to establish control over the police force. Above all, they had to beat Rol and the FFI in doing so.

Working through the *Honneur de la Police* and the *Police et Patrie*, Luizet organized the forcible takeover of the *préfecture de police* on the morning of August 19. At six that morning, a young policeman climbed on top of a car in the *préfecture's* courtyard and shouted, "In the name of General de Gaulle and the Provisional Government of the French Republic, I take possession of the *Préfecture de Police*." At the same time, some fifteen hundred to two thousand policemen waiting outside rushed into the courtyard and began singing *La Marseillaise.* There was no resistance. The tricolor was raised above the building, and the insurrection had begun.

Luizet was sitting on the terrace at the café Les Deux Magots sipping a cup of coffee when a black police car drove up and a policeman approached. "*Monsieur le Prefect*, the Prefecture is taken. It is now under your orders. Your car awaits."[14] Luizet stepped into the second car and drove off to his new position as the head of the Paris police department. His plan had worked perfectly. The Gaullists had taken control of the Paris police and had done so bloodlessly.

Rol was taken by surprise. Riding his bicycle along the quai to his headquarters in the 19th Arrondissemement, he heard the *Marseillaise* from the *préfecture*. Curious about the singing, Rol rode to the building and tried to enter, but was rebuffed by the guards. Going to a nearby garage, he changed into his Spanish Civil War uniform, which he had carried with him, and returned. He was greeted with a salute and escorted upstairs, where he met with the new *Comité de la Libération de la Police*. After a brief discussion, the police agreed to wear an FFI armband to show they were part of the Paris Resistance, and Rol was driven by the police to his headquarters.

That afternoon the leaders of the Resistance met to weigh the pros and cons of launching the insurrection. Parodi accused the Communists of beginning the revolt prematurely. André Tollet, the senior Communist present, pointed out that if the insurrection had begun, it was because of the Gaullist seizure of police headquarters. Eventually, the heated discussion became practical and the two sides came together. Using the authority entrusted to him by de Gaulle, Parodi issued orders for the mobilization of all Resistance members eighteen to fifty years old. He also placed all Resistance fighters under Rol and the FFI. Better unity than division. Rol had the necessary command structure to handle the insurrection, and it was best to join forces. The orders concluded with the words "Vive de Gaulle. Vive la France." Both sides had come together. "If I have made a mistake," said Parodi, "I shall have a lifetime to regret it in the ruins of Paris." [15]

While the Resistance leaders were meeting, the situation at the *préfecture de police* had turned ugly. German forces, including tanks and armored vehicles, had the building surrounded, and had begun a limited attack, but held off on a full-fledged assault. The iron entrance to the *préfecture* doors had been blown off, but the tanks had stopped short of trying to enter. Inside the *préfecture*, there was a growing recognition that if the Germans launched a full attack, they would prevail. One policeman called his wife. "This is all going badly. We will probably never see each other again." [16] And the police also found themselves short of ammunition.

Into the breach stepped Raoul Nordling, who correctly feared the massacre of the police inside the building if the Germans launched a major attack. In the afternoon Nordling went to the *préfecture* and spoke with Luizet. The two agreed that Nordling should see von Choltitz and try to work out a truce. Nordling immediately went to see von Choltitz at the Hotel Meurice. The meeting proved decisive. It was clear that von Choltitz did not want the fighting to escalate, but at the same time needed assurance that the violence would end. "It is against my men they shoot," he told Nordling.[17] Nordling pointed out that the FFI was primarily involved in fighting the Vichy forces and that the Germans were in the middle. Von Choltitz by this point knew the German army was on its way east, and that Paris could not be defended. He did not want to destroy the city, but needed a truce so that his forces would be preserved. Nordling left the meeting convinced that he could work out a truce that would end the fighting at the *préfecture*.

For the next several hours, Nordling negotiated with von Choltitz and Luizet by telephone. By 9 p.m. he had the terms in place. Von Choltitz would recognize the FFI as regular combatants, and agreed that the Germans would not fire on any building that was occupied by the police or the Resistance. In return, the French agreed not to attack any German installation or disrupt the movement of German troops through the city. For Nordling, it was an amazing diplomatic achievement. Not only had he saved the lives of the police officers in the *préfecture* and the buildings from destruction, but the truce also recognized the FFI as a legitimate negotiating partner. Von Choltitz faced the danger that if the truce became widely known, he could be relieved of command and arrested for negotiating with the enemy without approval from higher authority. For that reason the truce was not broadcast over the radio, but rather was announced by printed notices and loudspeaker trucks that moved through the city.

The truce saved the police, but was not universally respected. Neither the FFI nor the SS recognized it, and both remained in action. Rol especially was against it. "As long as the Germans are in Paris," he said, "it is our duty to fight them."[18] The Communists also rejected it. Said André Tollet, "The enemy is on the run. Why accept a truce? We have nothing to gain."[19] But the Gaullists were very much in favor. Chaban-Delmas understood that disagreement over the truce might split the Resistance, but thought it would give several more days for the Allies to get to Paris, when the Resistance could prevail. Unlike Rol, he recognized that the Germans could crush the Resistance if they decided to do so.

Sunday, August 20, was relatively quiet. There was minor fighting in the Latin Quarter, but for the most part it was a normal Sunday. One exception was the seizure of the Hôtel de Ville, the traditional seat of the Paris government, by a small group of policemen led by Leo Hamm, editor of the clandestine newspaper *Combat*. The prefect was arrested, as was Mayor Pierre Taittinger and the entire Paris City Council. But thus far, the casualties of the revolt had been relatively low. The best estimates are that 231 Frenchmen had been killed and some 800 wounded. German losses were somewhat fewer. The Gaullists now held not only the *préfecture de police*, but the Hôtel de Ville as well. With the truce in effect, Gaullists would move to occupy the various ministries of

L'Hôtel de Ville

the French government. As one scholar of the period has written, "It was a coup within a coup." [20] While Rol and the FFI engaged in various street battles throughout the city, the Gaullists seized the major government installations.

One of the most significant was the Hôtel Matignon, the official residence of the French prime minister and the Paris headquarters of Pierre Laval. Parodi decided to occupy it to give status and prestige to the Gaullist movement. On the spur of the moment, he sent his young assistant Yves Morandat and his secretary Claire Walborn to do the job. If there is opposition, said Parodi, leave the area immediately. "If there is opposition," Morandat replied, "I'll leave in a coffin." [21]

Not being Parisians, Morandat and Walborn did not know where the Hôtel Matignon was, and after bumbling their way around Paris on bicycles, they eventually came to it on the Rue de Varenne, across the Seine and deep on the Left Bank. Wearing the tricolor armbands of the FFI, they approached the heavily guarded entrance and told the sentry they had come to see the commander. They were escorted past more than a hundred guards in crisp black uniforms in the courtyard. "What do you want?" asked the commander.

"I have come to occupy these premises in the name of the Provisional Government of the French Republic," Morandat replied.

The commander called the guard to attention. "At your orders," he said. "I have always been a firm republican." [22] Laval had departed Paris several days before, and the Hôtel Matignon became a seat of de Gaulle's government.

Later that day, Parodi presided over a meeting of de Gaulle's ministers in the office of the prime minister—an office Laval had used the week before. The meeting dealt with the food problem in Paris, unemployment, and the need to establish order in the city. No decisions were made, but the fact that the ministers of the

Provisional Government were meeting in Paris was widely noted. Paris newspapers carried the story and overwhelmingly announced their support. That was important because the Gaullists needed public support, particularly from the left. Rol and the FFI said nothing. That too was significant. They did not endorse, but they did not oppose. They were focused on fighting the Germans, not on seizing power.

And the fighting on the streets of Paris continued, as the FFI and the SS continued to ignore the truce. At Rol's urging, the people of Paris took to the streets and began constructing barricades. Chaban-Delmas and the Gaullists went along, because the truce with von Choltitz said nothing about barricades. And barricades were a distinct feature of Paris's history. The revolutions of 1789 and 1848 had featured Paris barricades, and they were memorialized in *Les Miserables*, Victor Hugo's novel of the failed 1832 revolution. Within two days, some four hundred street barricades had been constructed. Most were built with paving stones from the roads, buttressed by disabled vehicles, felled trees, and sandbags. The barricades served no useful military purpose. If the Germans wished, they could have destroyed them with a couple of 88 mm shells. But they had an important symbolic value. They encouraged Parisians—male and female, young and old—to take part in the Resistance, as well as suggesting that the people of Paris controlled the streets. For the first time in four years, the people of the city were coming together. One Parisian noted that the barricades were not really aimed at the Germans but were "a matter between us and our long humiliation."[23]

And just as von Choltitz had done, many in the Resistance now looked for Allied intervention. Dr. Robert Monod, a leading Paris physician, devised a plan to seek help. On August 20, Monod wrote, "We have to prepare for a German offensive. Tomorrow the battle will resume and be much more violent."[24]

Monod thought the Germans were using the truce to prepare for a major attack and that what the Resistance needed most was the arrival of Allied soldiers. Monod wrote to Colonel Rol outlining a plan to move through German lines and urge the Americans to come as soon as possible. Monod suggested that he could handle the mission but he needed help. At 6 p.m. on the 20th, Rol's chief of staff, Major Roger Cocteau, codename Gallois, appeared at Monod's apartment and said that Rol agreed with the idea, and that he, Gallois, was going to accompany Monod. Gallois spoke English fluently, and ironically he and Monod were old friends. But there was a problem. Rol wanted the mission to ask the Americans to drop weapons for the Resistance. According to Gallois, Rol believed that the Americans could not get to Paris in time to help, and that the Parisians needed to liberate themselves.

Monod and Gallois left Paris at five the next morning, August 21. As a surgeon Monod had access to gasoline and a pass to allow passage through German lines. The cover story was that they were going to a hospital in Saint Nom de Bretéche, a small village close to the front lines. Monod had attended patients there previously, and Gallois would pose as his male nurse. The route to the village was circuitous, and on the way Monod convinced Gallois that what was needed was not weapons but Allied forces. At the hospital, they met an FFI contact codenamed Georges who agreed to take Gallois to the Americans. Monod did not accompany Gallois further and returned to his duties in Paris.

Georges drove Gallois to the front lines, where the opposing troops were not far apart. Gallois crawled through the woods where the Germans were dug in. He believed they saw him but did not fire on him because they did not want to attract American attention. He crossed into American lines at roughly 7:30 p.m. on August 21. The American soldiers were dumbfounded. After a brief exchange he was driven in a jeep to regimental headquarters, where he was interrogated extensively by Colonel Robert Powell, who spoke French and specialized in the French Resistance. After several hours of intense interrogation the colonel was satisfied Gallois was who he said he was, and he was whisked off for another lengthy jeep ride to Third Army headquarters. By then it was after midnight, and Gallois was interrogated once again, this time by Colonel Harold Lyon, the commander of the T-Force General Bradley had established to move into Paris and secure scientific and industrial targets quickly if the situation required it. Lyon was also satisfied Gallois was credible. As he summarized it, Gallois had provided five important pieces of information: the Paris police were on strike; barricades were being constructed throughout the city; the FFI was in control of many areas; the German high command had agreed to a truce; and the truce would expire shortly. Colonel Lyon concluded that the situation in Paris "was an opportunity which the Allies had to take advantage of immediately." [25]

It was now 1:30 a.m. on August 22, and Gallois was exceedingly tired. But the staff at Third Army headquarters thought the situation required action. General Patton was awakened and soon came in to see Gallois. "O.K. I'm listening. What's your story?" he asked. Gallois repeated his story as carefully as he could. When he finished, Patton replied: "You are a soldier, and I'm a soldier. I'm going to answer you as a soldier." He said the answer was no, for three reasons. The Allies, said Patton, were "destroying Germans, not capturing capitals"; the Resistance had started the insurrection without orders; and the Allies, who were short of gasoline, could not "accept the moral responsibility of feeding the city." [26] Patton continued:

> You ought to know that our operations at this moment were not conceived lightly. We are obliged to follow our plans to the letter and not even a fortuitous or unexpected event like this one can change these plans, even if the event is of such

extraordinary importance. Our objective is Berlin and we want to end this war as quickly as possible. The immediate capture of Paris is not part of the plan. . . . You should have waited for orders from Allied headquarters before launching an insurrection and not taken the initiative yourselves.[27]

Patton shook Gallois's hand and left the room. Gallois was crestfallen. It was, he said later, the most depressing moment in his life. He was "in a state of emotional collapse."[28] Suddenly Patton returned. He was carrying a bottle of champagne and two glasses. He offered a stunned Gallois a toast to victory. After drinking it down, he said to Gallois, "Are you ready to take a long voyage?"[29] There was another general, Patton said, whom Gallois should see. Patton had had a change of heart. At 3:30 a.m. Gallois got into a jeep and was driven off. Patton had arranged for him to see General Bradley.

— VI —

Eisenhower Changes Plans

"What the hell, Brad, I guess we will have to go in."

—EISENHOWER TO BRADLEY, AUGUST 22, 1944

Eisenhower knew Paris and appreciated its cultural uniqueness and political significance. Unlike other American and British generals, or Roosevelt and Churchill for that matter, Ike had lived in Paris for fourteen months in the late 1920s. Assigned to General John J. Pershing's Battle Monuments Commission in July 1928, Eisenhower remained in Paris until August 1929. And he enjoyed every minute. As he and Mamie said later, the time in Paris was the most idyllic period in their marriage. "We had a nice life and a nice group of friends. Our son, John, was going to a good school, and we had lots of fun and lots of company."[1]

Paris in the late twenties was a mecca for many Americans. The free-spiritedness, the absence of Prohibition, and a very favorable exchange rate made it a perfect place for Americans to enjoy life. Ernest Hemingway captured the mood when he wrote, "Paris in the winter is rainy, cold, beautiful, and cheap. It is also noisy, jostling, crowded, and cheap. It is anything you want—and cheap."[2]

The Eisenhowers lived in a very fashionable residence in the 16th Arrondissement, overlooking the Seine and the Pont Mira-

111

Eisenhower, fifth from right, marching with General Pershing's staff at the Paris funeral of Marshal Ferdinand Foch, March 20, 1929

beau.* Eisenhower studied French daily, became proficient in reading and writing it, but was never able to speak it without a pronounced Midwestern accent. They entertained frequently at home, and also in the elegant officers' club, the *Cercle de l'Union Interalliée*, next to the Elysée Palace on the fashionable Faubourg Saint-Honoré. Eisenhower revised the army's guidebook to World War I battlefields for American tourists, and helped Pershing write his memoirs. He marched in the funeral parade for Marshal Ferdinand Foch on March 20, 1929, and took an interest in French politics.

---

* The Eisenhower apartment was owned by the Comtesse de Villefranche, the doyenne of one of France's most distinguished families, and was on the premier floor at 68 Quai d'Auteuil. It contained a large vestibule, two sitting rooms, a dining room, three bedrooms, an immense kitchen, and quarters for the help in the attic. It was elegantly furnished, and as Mamie once said, as far from typical army quarters "as were Peary and Amundsen when they reached their respective poles." Alden Hatch, *Red Carpet for Mamie* (New York: Henry Holt, 1954), 150.

It was his study of French politics in the late twenties that helped explain Eisenhower's attachment to de Gaulle. Unlike in the United States, the French did not agree on the rules of the political game. Since 1789 there had been three republics, three monarchies, two empires, the Paris Commune, and the Vichy Regime.* Ike understood that the French Revolution, unlike the American Revolution, was a civil war, and that the outcome was still being contested. The radical right and the Church rejected the republic, and the republic rejected Christianity and the Church. The principal party during the Third Republic was the Radical-Socialists, which was neither radical nor socialist but a middle-class party dedicated to the secularization of France. The issues dividing the country were intractable, and Eisenhower recognized that to govern France effectively was very difficult.

After a year in Paris, Eisenhower became concerned that the Battle Monuments Commission was a career cul-de-sac, and that he was out of the army's mainstream. He contacted his guardian angel, General Fox Conner, and asked to be transferred. General Fox Conner played a major role in shaping Eisenhower's career.

---

* Following the fall of the Bastille on July 14, 1789, France experimented with a constitutional monarchy for three years. Louis XVI remained on the throne with his power curtailed. But in 1792 he was deposed and executed, and the First Republic was established. Napoléon overthrew the Republic in 1799 and proclaimed the French Empire. The Bourbon Monarchy was restored in 1814, and was overthrown by the constitutional monarchy of the duc d'Orléans, Louis-Philippe in 1830. The Revolution of 1848 toppled the Orleanist monarchy and established the Second Republic, which ruled France until 1852, when Louis-Napoléon Bonaparte (Napoléon's nephew) mounted a coup and established the Second Empire. Napoléon III (as he was styled) ruled France until Germany's 1871 victory in the Franco-Prussian War. A period of instability ensued, dominated by the Paris Commune of 1871, a legendary benchmark for the Marxist Left. The provisional government of Adolphe Thiers followed, and the Third Republic was ushered in in 1875. The Third Republic, which Eisenhower was familiar with from the twenties, was always under attack from the monarchist Right and the antidemocratic Left, heirs to the spirit of the Commune.

In 1921, when Ike was threatened with court-martial for drawing a housing allowance for his son "Ikey," who was not with him at the time, Conner intervened and the charges were dropped. From 1921 to 1924, Eisenhower served as Conner's executive officer in the Canal Zone, and they became close friends. In 1925 Eisenhower was passed over by the chief of infantry for attendance at the Army's Command and General Staff School at Fort Leavenworth. Conner intervened once again. Eisenhower was transferred to the Adjutant General's Corps and was admitted to Leavenworth on the AG's quota in August 1925. Ike finished first in his class at Leavenworth, but the chief of infantry, annoyed that Eisenhower had made an end run around him, assigned him to be executive officer in the black Twenty-Fourth Infantry Regiment at Fort Benning. The Twenty-Fourth Infantry, unlike the black Tenth Cavalry, was regarded as a funeral parlor for the white officers assigned. Once again Conner came to the rescue and Ike was reassigned. After just five months with the Twenty-Fourth, Eisenhower received orders transferring him to the Battle Monuments Commission. As Mamie Eisenhower said, "No man can make a successful career on his own. And Ike was fortunate to have sponsors like Fox Conner . . . who pushed him ahead." In 1930, Conner was on a short list of two to become the army's chief of staff, and was strongly backed by Pershing, but Herbert Hoover chose Douglas MacArthur instead. In 1935, FDR offered to make Conner chief of staff, but Conner, who was close to retirement, declined. Eisenhower later told Stephen Ambrose that "Fox Conner was the ablest man I ever knew. . . . In a lifetime of association with great and good men, he is the one to whom I owe an incalculable debt."[3]

Conner intervened, and on August 10, 1929, Eisenhower received orders transferring him to the War Department, where he would become military assistant to the assistant secretary of war. It was most unusual for someone with an overseas assignment to be transferred back to the United States before it ended, but Conner had arranged it.*

Eisenhower's time in Paris provided him with the necessary understanding to appreciate de Gaulle's insistence that Paris be liberated without delay. He recognized that Paris was not just a capital city, but the center of French life. Whoever controlled Paris controlled France, and it was essential that it be in friendly hands. The inhabitants of Paris also had to be saved from civil war and a new Paris Commune. And if the monuments of Paris could be preserved, it was important to do so. The Germans were holding off, but could do so only for a limited time. And the truce that von Choltitz had agreed to would expire shortly. Also, the plan to bypass Paris had been prepared by the Allied staff in London before D-Day, not by Eisenhower.[4] It made military sense, in that street fighting in Paris would delay the Allied advance, and the logistical burden of supplying food and fuel to a city of four million would be an incredible burden. But it ignored an important political reality. As in North Africa with the Darlan affair, Eisenhower realized that staff planners were often unfamiliar with the political needs of the military.[5]

On August 21, the day after their meeting, de Gaulle sent an urgent letter to Eisenhower pressing for immediate action. The letter was delivered personally by General Koenig, who provided additional details of the situation in Paris. Wrote de Gaulle:

---

* Major Xenophon Price, Pershing's executive officer, gave Eisenhower a final efficiency report of "satisfactory." (His previous reports had all been "superior.") Price said that Ike "was not especially versitile [Price's spelling] in adjusting to changed conditions." It was Eisenhower's lowest efficiency rating since 1917. After the war, when Eisenhower became chief of staff, he inquired what had happened to Price. It turned out he was still on active duty with the Corps of Engineers, in the rank of lieutenant colonel. Eisenhower was shocked. "Why was he only a lieutenant colonel," Ike asked. "Bad judgment" came the reply. "Hell, he's not that bad," said Eisenhower and ordered him promoted to colonel. Letter, John S. D. Eisenhower to JES, March 10, 2008.

The information which I received today from PARIS leads me to believe that owing to the nearly complete disappearance of the police forces and the German forces from PARIS, and the present extreme shortage of food which exists, that serious trouble must be foreseen in the Capital within a short time.

I believe that it is really necessary to occupy PARIS as soon as possible with French and Allied forces, even if it should produce some fighting and some damage within the City.

If disorder now occurs in PARIS, it will later be difficult to take things in hand without serious incidents that could, in my opinion, ultimately hinder future military operations.

I am sending General KOENIG to you, nominated Military Governor of PARIS and Commandant of the Region of Paris, to confer with you on the question of occupation in case you decide to proceed without delay.

Very cordially yours,
C. de Gaulle[6]

Eisenhower read de Gaulle's letter carefully, and he listened to Koenig. It was clear that Paris could become a seat of revolution, and that another commune might be established. The need to go into Paris immediately was apparent. But to do so, Eisenhower needed the approval or at least the acquiescence of his superiors, the Combined Chiefs of Staff. He immediately wrote a very lengthy cable disguising his decision, but placing it before the Chiefs. To ease the matter, he talked about the liberation of Paris only in passing.

I have reprinted Eisenhower's cable of August 22 in its entirety to illustrate how skillful Ike was in disguising his decision. Paris was primarily a political and humanitarian issue, and Ike understood that he had to conceal that. Accordingly, the cable dealt with the overall military situation in France. Paris was a marginal issue. But it was the most telling portion of the message. I have italicized those portions dealing with Paris.

TOP SECRET

This is a personal report to the Combined Chiefs of Staff.

The time is approaching when there will be put into effect the final system of Command as planned from the beginning for this operation. The exact date of initiating the final phase will be determined by possibilities in establishing on the Continent the communications needed by the operational sections of SHAEF Headquarters, accompanied by Operational Sections of the NAVAL and AIR Headquarters. The target date is September 1st, by which time the remaining elements of the enemy south of the SEINE and west of PARIS should have been destroyed and possibly crossings secured over that River.

As arranged during April, the Tactical Air Force, The United States Strategic Air Force and the Bomber Command each report independently to the Supreme Commander, who uses his Deputy to assist in the coordination of the activities of these 3 Forces. There will be no change in this general system except that the Commander of the Tactical Air Forces, together with representatives of the Day and Night Bomber Forces will be with the Supreme Commander in FRANCE.

On the ground, the responsibility of the Commander in Chief, 21 Army Group, in arranging for coordination between the 21st and 12 Army Groups, will terminate coincidentally with the establishment of SHAEF on the Continent. At that time the 21st Army Group, which in this Command will be designated the Army Group of the North, will operate to the northeastward, securing successive bases along the coast with its final base possibly ANTWERP. Eventually it will be directed to advance eastward generally north of the ARDENNES. The 21st Army Group will probably be reinforced by the entire Airborne Command and by such other units as are necessary to enable it to accomplish its first and immediately important mission, which will be to destroy forces lying between the SEINE and PAS DE CALAIS, and to occupy that area.

The Army Group of the center, less portions necessarily employed otherwise, as indicated in this report, will advance, under General BRADLEY, to the east and northeast of PARIS, from which area it can either strike northeastward, thus assisting in the rapid fall of the CALAIS area and the later advance through the Low Countries, or, if the enemy strength in that region is not greater than I now believe, it can alternatively strike directly eastward, passing south of the ARDENNES. The speed of BRADLEY'S advance to the region east of PARIS will be governed by the speed at which the ports in BRITTANY can be cleaned up, and our supply situation improved. Depending on this it may prove possible for BRADLEY to thrust a mobile column southeast to create an additional threat, and speed up the rate of advance of DRAGOON. *Because of the additional supply commitments incurred in the occupation of PARIS it would be desirable from that viewpoint, to defer the capture of the city until the important matter of destroying the remaining enemy forces up to include the PAS DE CALAIS area. I do not believe this is possible. If the enemy tries to hold PARIS with any real strength he would be a constant menace to our flank. If he largely evacuates the place, it falls into our hands whether we like it or not.*

When the Army Group of the South has advanced sufficiently far that the Combined Chiefs of Staff place responsibility for its control in the hands of this Headquarters it will continue to maneuver to support the advance of the Army Group of the Center.

Each of these Army Groups will be accompanied by its own Tactical Air Force, comprised of mainly fighter, fighter bombers, and light bombers and reconnaissance units. Heavier types of airplanes will be centrally controlled, so as to be available when necessary, for the support of any one of the 3 Army Groups. In this connection, it is my conviction that the time has now come for the Strategic Force to resume maximum pressure against targets in GERMANY and this policy has been approved. Strategic Day and Night Forces will be diverted from that mission, only when the immediate requirements of the battle so demand. Naturally these forces will continue to blast Crossbow sites.

There will no change in the Naval Command, except that the Naval Commander in Chief will be located in FRANCE.

It is possible that some Airborne Troops may have to be used at an early date, to assist in gaining crossings over the SEINE but I would regard this use as undesirable and do not believe that we will have to do so. My hope is to preserve the full Airborne Command intact to be used in one great operation with the Army Group of the North in seizing CALAIS area and destroying enemy forces there. Afterward it will be recollected for use in advancing on GERMANY. In this connection the Air Transport Command (less detachments in the Mediterranean) is currently being used to help supply the marching wing of the 12 Army Group whose maintenance has been stretched to the limit. Two Corps of this Army Group are now being employed to thrust north and northwest from the general area DREUX-MAULETTE toward EVREUX-LOUVIERS to assist in trapping the army still west of the SEINE while 21 Army Group maintains direct pressure. Currently also, the Forces in BRITTANY are being reinforced so as to bring about the rapid capture of BREST and the ports on the southern coast of the Peninsula. I repeat that it is absolutely mandatory for us to clean up our maintenance situation on the southern flank.

I desire to report that our Command system has functioned exactly as planned and in accordance with the developments of the tactical and strategic situation. No hitches have occurred and no frictions that I know of have developed. On the contrary, in spite of the difficult situation that always come about with overseas landings and the establishment of new theater of operations, the whole command has operated smoothly and effectively. For this the credit is due to the Commanders in Chief, to all other Senior Commanders and to the Higher Staff of all Services. The final stage in Command is becoming necessary because of somewhat diverging lines of operation and because on each of the main fronts there must be a Commander who can handle, with a reasonable degree of independence, the day by day detailed operations of troops, guided by the overall directives prescribed by this Headquarters.

When PARIS is entered, it is my intention to employ the French Division for occupation. In entering the city it will be accompanied by Token Units of British and American forces. Some days thereafter, General DE GAULLE will be allowed to make his formal entry into the city. I will not personally go there until military considerations require.[7]

By stressing that Paris could become "a constant menace in our flank," Eisenhower was presenting a military justification for taking Paris. And by concluding with a reference to Paris as a fait accompli, he was removing the issue from debate. Eisenhower was covering his tracks, and he was very good at doing this. He did not write to General Marshall, who commanded all American forces, but to the Combined Chiefs of Staff. That would make it more difficult to overrule him. He had decided to liberate Paris, and would allow de Gaulle to reap the benefits. This was a political decision. The best parallel in American history is Ulysses Grant at Appomattox in 1865, where on his own authority he pardoned all members of the Confederate army who returned home and abided by the laws in place where they resided. Eisenhower understood the importance of Paris, and that was all that was required.

He also knew Bradley was opposed to taking Paris. As Bradley wrote in his memoirs, everyone wanted to liberate Paris. "Everybody, that is, except me. In a tactical sense Paris was meaningless. We were in pursuit of the fleeing German Army, which was leaving Paris behind. It had always been our plan to bypass Paris, isolating whatever garrison troops it might contain, and deal with it after we had destroyed the German Army or, at least, reached the Siegfried Line on the Rhine. Pausing to liberate Paris would not only needlessly slow our eastward drive, but also require the diversion of transport and gasoline to provide for four million Parisians a planned 4,000 tons of food and supplies per day."[8]

Eisenhower immediately sent for Bradley to inform him of his decision. At almost the same time, Roger Gallois of the Paris Resistance arrived at Bradley's headquarters in Laval. Gallois did not see Bradley, but in the hour before Bradley departed to see Ike, Gallois spoke at length with Brigadier General Edwin Sibert, Twelfth Army Group's intelligence chief (G-2). Gallois

General Omar Bradley

was fatigued after his three jeep journeys that night but rallied to the occasion. "The people of Paris wanted to liberate their capital themselves," he said, "but they cannot finish what they have started. You must come to our help, or there is going to be a terrible slaughter. Hundreds of thousands of Frenchmen are going to be killed." Gallois's presentation was impressive. Sibert, who would accompany Bradley to Ike's headquarters, was profoundly impressed by what he had heard. On the flight to see Eisenhower, Sibert briefed Bradley on Gallois's presentation. "If we don't get to Paris in a couple of days, there's going to be an awful massacre."[9]

Bradley arrived at Eisenhower's headquarters in Tourniers at about 10 a.m. on August 22. As a result of Sibert's briefing, Bradley already recognized that Paris had to be liberated. The discussion with Ike was brief. Koenig and Juin also took part. "What the hell, Brad, I guess we have to go in," said Eisenhower.[10] He then instructed Bradley to use Leclerc's Second Armored Division to lead the way, and said he had ordered twenty-three thousand tons of food and three thousand tons of coal to be dispatched to Paris immediately. "No great battle is going to take place," said Eisenhower, and "the entry of one or two divisions would accomplish the liberation of the city."[11]

The decision had been made. It was a breathtaking decision that Eisenhower intentionally understated. In his memoirs, Ike does not mention his meeting with de Gaulle on August 20, or de Gaulle's letter of the 21st. He is careful to place his decision to take Paris strictly in military terms. Later that day he penned a note on de Gaulle's letter for his chief of staff, Walter Bedell Smith. "I talked verbally to KOENIG on this. It looks now as if we'd be compelled to go into Paris. BRADLEY and his G-2 think we can and *must* walk in."[12]

Bradley understood the importance of Eisenhower's decision to take Paris and accepted it as his own. After the meeting with Ike, he flew to First Army headquarters. He arrived at 2 p.m. on August 22, and briefed General Courtney Hodges and his staff on the change in plans. "Paris can be avoided no longer," said Bradley, and General Leclerc's division was to lead the way. Hodges and his staff were taken by surprise, but adjusted quickly. As one staff member recalls, "The corps staff assembled in the war room . . . [followed by] the hasty assembling of maps, the hurried writing of movement orders, the determination of routes of march . . . [and] the careful instructions to the French, who have a casual manner of doing almost exactly what they please, regardless of orders."[13]

After briefing First Army, Bradley flew to Laval, where Leclerc was waiting. He arrived at 7:15 p.m. on August 22. With Leclerc was Roger Gallois, the messenger from Paris. Leclerc rushed to board the plane before Bradley deplaned. "You win," said General Sibert. "They've decided to send you to Paris." Bradley then deplaned and spoke to both Leclerc and Gallois. "The decision has been made to enter Paris, and the three of us share in the responsibility for it. I, because I have given the order; you, General Leclerc, because you are going to execute it; and you, Major Gallois, because it was largely on the basis of the information you brought that the decision was made."[14]

Bradley then laid out his orders to Leclerc in detail. "Paris was to be entered only if the degree of fighting could be overcome by light forces." He was not to use artillery or air support inside Paris, and if he encountered heavy German resistance he should retreat and await reinforcements. Once inside Paris, he was to relieve the FFI and assume responsibility for security in the city. This should be done as soon as possible.[15]

Eisenhower had made the decision to liberate Paris and Bradley was implementing it. They were further encouraged on the evening of August 23, when von Choltitz's messengers arrived. Swedish consul Raoul Nordling had begun to organize his trip into Allied lines immediately after von Choltitz suggested he do so. That was in the morning of August 22. But that afternoon, before he could leave, Nordling suffered a mild heart attack that immobilized him. He asked his brother Rolf to take his place, which he did. In addition to Rolf Nordling, the party that left Paris on August 22 included Alexandre de Saint-Phalle as the representative of the Committee of National Liberation; Max Armoux, ostensibly from the Red Cross but actually from British Intelligence; and Erich Posch-Pastor von Camperfeld, an Austrian spy who had provided valuable information to the Allies. Von Choltitz added

Emil "Bobby" Bender to the group, an intelligence agent in Paris whom he trusted to help Nordling through German lines.

The group made it through Versailles on the road to American lines, but when they hit the village of Trappes, they were halted by German SS sentries. The captain in charge looked at the orders von Choltitz had written and then dismissed them. "Since the 20th of July we don't obey Wehrmacht generals," he said. Bender flew into a rage, and it was finally agreed that they would return to Versailles, where the orders could be confirmed. Bender called von Choltitz, who gave a direct order to the SS *Hauptsturmführer* to let them through. If the officer failed to clear the party through his lines, said von Choltitz, "I will come out and see it's done." The car was allowed to proceed, but soon ran into a German minefield. They were led through by a German sentry, who at the end of the field pointed west and said, "The Americans. Five hundred meters." [16]

Von Choltitz's messengers went through the same labyrinth as Gallois. They were taken to Patton, who, as in his initial reception of Gallois, was grim. In his diary Patton wrote, "The brother of the Swedish Consul in Paris, a man named Ralf [sic] Nordling and a group of other French individuals from Paris were in camp with a proposition. I immediately thought that they might be asking for a surrender. . . . It turned out that these people simply wanted to get a suspension of hostilities in order to save Paris, and probably save some Germans. I sent them to see Bradley." [17]

Like Gallois earlier, they met Bradley on the airstrip in Laval. Bradley listened intently as Nordling told him that von Choltitz had "formal orders" to destroy as much of Paris as possible. He had not done so, but he was "being backed into a corner," and if the situation didn't change quickly, he would have to execute the orders. There was also the possibility that he would be relieved of command. What he needed was for the Allies to come as soon as possible.

Bradley heard Nordling out. And he reacted immediately. The operation that Ike had ordered yesterday needed to be speeded up. "We can't take any chances," he said. Bradley told General Sibert to "tell Hodges to have the French division hurry the hell in there." And recognizing how far Leclerc had to go, Bradley made another decision. "Tell him to have the 4th Division ready to get in there too. We can't take any chances on that general changing his mind and knocking hell out of the city." [18]

Eisenhower on his own authority had changed plans and was going to liberate Paris. It was clear to him what had to be done. It was also clear that he had to cast this as a military issue, not a political or humanitarian one, and that he must maintain a low profile and leave it up to the French. Eisenhower's decision to liberate Paris was one of the great decisions of World War II. And it was not without cost. By diverting supplies and fuel to the French capital, he undoubtedly prolonged the war. But he avoided another Paris Commune in return.

Eisenhower's political skill, like that of General Grant, set him apart from most military commanders. It was long-standing and had been carefully developed. At West Point, he was the most popular cadet in his class. In the early twenties in Panama under Fox Conner he had learned how to command, and directly underneath MacArthur from 1931 until 1939 he learned how military commanders deal with their civilian bosses. In fact in 1938 a group of Philippine legislators had sought to abolish MacArthur's job and leave Eisenhower in charge.* Marshall recognized Ike's

---

* "I was familiar with the details," said General Lucius D. Clay. "A group in the Philippine legislature decided Eisenhower was doing all the work and that he was being paid only $10,000 a year, whereas MacArthur was being given a beautiful penthouse

political skill when he brought him to Washington after Pearl Harbor, and in North Africa Eisenhower not only brought the American and British military forces together, but also carefully overturned the State Department and FDR's attempt to manage liberated French territory through Vichy agents. His ties to de Gaulle trace to that, and Eisenhower understood the need to play this situation close to his chest.

---

apartment in the Manila Hotel and being paid a much more substantial sum. This little group of Filipino congressmen prepared to introduce a bill that would abolish the top job—MacArthur's job—and leave Eisenhower in charge. When Eisenhower heard about it, he went to them and told them that if they ever introduced such a bill he would immediately ask to be returned to the United States. That under no circumstances would he be a party to it. But General MacArthur found out about it. From that moment on he had no more use for Eisenhower. And it was absolutely unfounded, although I am sure there were people who deliberately tried to convince MacArthur that Eisenhower was trying to knife him in the back." Lucius D. Clay interview, April 21, 1971, in Jean Edward Smith, *Lucius D. Clay: An American Life* (New York: Henry Holt, 1990), 80–81.

— VII —

Leclerc Moves Out

"Gribius, mouvement immédiat sur Paris."

—LECLERC TO MAJOR ANDRÉ GRIBIUS, AUGUST 22, 1944

The French Second Armored Division, which General Jacques Leclerc commanded, landed in France on August 1, 1944—almost two months after D-Day. It was assigned to George Patton's Third Army, and Leclerc and Patton got along well. Patton spoke French and offered Leclerc the opportunity to go into battle immediately instead of waiting to liberate Paris. Leclerc jumped at the offer, and Patton assigned him to XV Corps, commanded by General Wade Haislip. Haislip had studied at the École de Guerre in Paris and was also fluent in French. Leclerc hit it off well with both Patton and Haislip, and in the battle of the Falaise Pocket, the Second Armored Division played a major role. But before the Germans surrendered, Patton sent most of Haislip's corps eastward toward the Seine. Leclerc's division was kept on line to contain the German forces.

Leclerc was perplexed why his division had remained on line while most of XV Corps went eastward. He immediately sought out Patton and asked when his division could go to Paris. "It is political," he said.[1] Patton said he needed Leclerc to stay put to contain the Germans, and dismissed his query. On August 15, Patton wrote in his diary, "Leclerc came in very much excited. He said, among other things, that if he were not allowed to advance on Paris, he would resign. I told him in my best French that he was a baby and . . . that I had left him in the most dangerous place. We parted friends."[2] The following day Leclerc wrote Patton that everything was quiet at Argentan, and said it was probably time for him to regroup to move toward Paris. That evening he went to Patton's headquarters to repeat his plea. General Bradley was there, and both he and Patton assured Leclerc that they would allow him to liberate Paris, but it was not yet time to do so. At this point, Haislip's corps was on the Seine some thirty-five miles from Paris. Leclerc was understandably skeptical of their response.

With the bulk of XV Corps on the Seine and Patton moving eastward, Leclerc found himself suddenly transferred from Third Army to First Army, commanded by Lieutenant General Courtney Hodges. Hodges assigned the French Second Armored Division to V Corps, commanded by Major General Leonard Gerow. Gerow had commanded the landing on Omaha Beach and had been in combat ever since. Neither Hodges nor Gerow spoke French, and neither seemed to appreciate the importance Leclerc placed on the liberation of Paris and the special role his division was to play. When Leclerc pressed the point, Gerow dismissed the idea and said that Paris was no particular concern of his. The Second Armored Division would be employed just like any American division under his command.[3]

On August 20, General Hodges invited Leclerc for lunch to become acquainted. Leclerc talked incessantly about Paris and argued that he should be allowed to head toward the city immediately. Hodges was not impressed and told Leclerc that he was to stay put until he received orders to move.

The next day, August 21, the Falaise Pocket closed, and Leclerc saw no further justification in remaining so far from Paris. That evening he decided that as the sole commander of French

General Leonard Gerow

forces in the Allied armies in France he was entitled to exercise his judgment when national issues were at stake. On his own authority he ordered a relatively small force of seventeen tanks, ten armored cars, and ten personnel carriers, under Lieutenant Colonel Jacques Guillebon, to head toward Paris. If the Allies decided to enter Paris without Leclerc's Second Armored Division, then Guillebon was to accompany the liberating troops as the representative of the French army and the Provisional Government. Leclerc informed de Gaulle that evening of what he had done and said he could not dispatch his whole division because food and fuel were furnished by the Americans and because of his respect for "the rules of military subordination."[4]

The following morning, August 22, Leclerc sent his G-2, Major Phillippe Repiton, to Gerow's headquarters to explain what he had done. The reason Leclerc provided was that the insurrection that was taking place in Paris made it necessary for an advance military detachment to get there and maintain order until the arrival of the French Provisional Government. Leclerc further pointed out that the absence of Guillebon's small force did not affect the ability of the Second Armored Division to fulfill any combat mission that V Corps might assign.

Gerow, who had been alerted earlier about the movement of Guillebon's force, was incensed at what he considered Leclerc's insubordination. Before Major Repiton could speak, Gerow presented him with a letter for Leclerc that he had just written. "I desire to make it clear to you that the 2nd Armored Division (French) is under my command for all purposes and no part of it will be employed by you except in the execution of missions assigned by this headquarters." He went on to order Leclerc to recall Guillebon.[5] Gerow, unlike Eisenhower, saw the liberation of Paris purely in military terms.*

———————

* Gerow's position is best understood by noting that he and Eisenhower were old friends, going back to 1915, when they both served as lieutenants in the Nineteenth Infantry, the famous "Rock of Chickamauga" regiment, stationed at Fort Sam Houston, Texas. In the mid-1920s they were classmates and study partners at the Command and General Staff School at Fort Leavenworth. Eisenhower graduated first in the class of 224, and Gerow finished second. In the early thirties both were in Washington at the War Department and both lived in the Wyoming apartment building until Ike went to Manila with MacArthur. In November of 1940 Gerow, who had become head of War Plans in the War Department, sought to have Eisenhower appointed his deputy but withdrew the request when Ike expressed his desire to remain with troops. Finally, in December 1941, after Pearl Harbor, Marshall brought Eisenhower to the War Department and on February 14, 1942, eased Gerow out as head of War Plans and installed Ike. Gerow was promoted to Major General and given command of the Twenty-Ninth Infantry Division. In July 1943 he was named commander of V Corps, and played a major role in planning for the D-Day invasion. But his long-standing friendship with Eisenhower was most important. Gerow did not see the war in political terms, and that partially explains his dislike of Lerclerc.

Leclerc may have been unique among Allied commanders in Europe. The offspring of minor nobility in Picardy, he cultivated an air of mystery. A devout Catholic who received the Eucharist daily, he exhibited a mulish streak that often angered his superiors.[6] This was such an occasion. Rather than obey Gerow's order, he immediately flew to General Bradley's headquarters in Laval to appeal. When he arrived, he learned that Bradley was conferring with Eisenhower on Paris, and was expected to arrive shortly. Leclerc decided the best thing for him to do was to await Bradley's arrival. And when Bradley arrived, it was a new ball game. By Eisenhower's order, Paris was to be liberated and Leclerc's division was to lead the way. Leclerc was not only off the hook for his disobedience to Gerow, but he would lead the Allied advance. An overjoyed Leclerc returned immediately to his division. It was almost dark on the evening of August 22 when he arrived. He jumped from the plane and shouted to his waiting operations officer, Major André Gribius, *"Gribius, mouvement immédiat sur Paris."*[7]

The Second Armored Division was at Argentan in Normandy. Paris was 122 miles away. With 16,000 men, 200 Sherman tanks, 4,000 other vehicles, and more than 250 artillery pieces, Leclerc planned to be in Paris in two days. That evening he prepared for the move out, which he scheduled for dawn. To his men he said, "I demand, for this movement which will lead the Division to the capital of France, a supreme effort which I am sure to obtain from you all."[8] General Gerow called later that evening and instructed Leclerc to leave that night, but Leclerc, who was well aware of the route, decided it would be best to wait until daylight. The relationship between Gerow and Leclerc had been strained from the beginning. Gerow considered Leclerc his subordinate; Leclerc believed his commanders were Bradley, Eisenhower, and de Gaulle.

Leclerc's Second Armored Division set out at 6 a.m. on August

23. It split and took two routes. The northern route went through Sées and Mortagne to Rambouillet; the southern through Alençon, Chartres, and Limours. The bulk of the division, plus some American reconnaissance and engineer troops, and four howitzer battalions from V Corps artillery, took the northern route. The forces on the southern route consisted of a French combat command, Gerow and V Corps headquarters, and the U.S. Fourth Infantry Division. Both groups made good progress, reaching points roughly twenty-five miles from Paris by nightfall. No German units were encountered, and in every village the population turned out to see the troops advance. Veterans of past wars stood at attention snapping salutes, while cheering civilians tossed flowers and apples to the passing troops. Colonel David Bruce, the head of the OSS in France, said the troops "were offered beer, cider, white and red Bordeaux, white and red Burgundy, champagne, rum, whiskey, cognac, Armagnac, and calvados—enough to wreck one's constitution." Bruce, who later became President Truman's ambassador to France (May 1949–March 1952), admired Leclerc for his command style. "He is tall, spare, handsome, stern-visaged, and a striking figure. . . . Like the Scarlet Pimpernel he is said to have been seen here, there, and everywhere."[9]

At Rambouillet, Leclerc met de Gaulle, who had arrived somewhat earlier, and was ensconced in the Château de Rambouillet, a former residence of the kings of France. Leclerc was changing plans slightly and moving on Paris from the south, not through Versailles as Gerow had directed. Leclerc believed that the wide Orléans-Paris highway would be easier to navigate and would speed up his time of arrival. De Gaulle listened carefully and approved. He ordered Leclerc to establish his command post at the Gare Montparnasse when he arrived. "I would join him there in order to settle what to do next. Then, observing this young leader already at grips with the demands of battle, and whose valor was

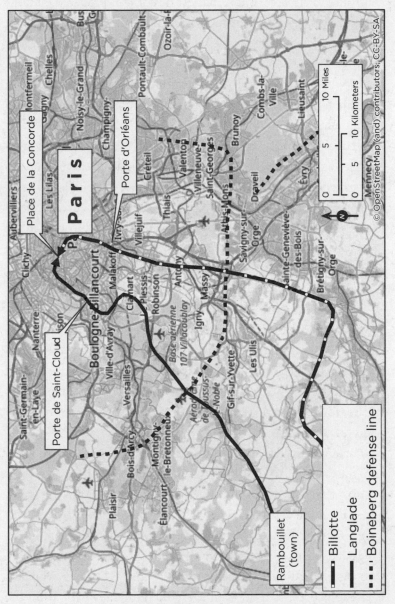

Figure 3: LeClerc's route to Paris

confronted with an extraordinary series of well-prepared circumstances, I murmured, 'How lucky you are.' And I also thought how in war the luck of the generals is the honor of governments."[10]

August 23, 1944, was also a day when the news of the Allied advance spread quickly. The BBC announced "Paris is free!" and the British War Cabinet ordered a thanksgiving service in St. Paul's Cathedral.[11] King George VI sent a telegram of congratulations to de Gaulle. Although the telegram was premature, de Gaulle was delighted since he believed it was "intended to force the Americans to renounce their ulterior motives which the English did not approve."[12] Foreign Secretary Anthony Eden said, "Every citizen of every free country has no doubt been moved by the news about Paris." And the lord mayor of London sent a telegram to General Koenig congratulating him on this "supreme moment of victory. A world without Paris is inconceivable."[13]

As Colonel Bruce reported, "A gush of Allied war correspondents poured into Rambouillet this morning," having been informed that Leclerc had been given the go-ahead. "The correspondents are furious with Leclerc," said Bruce, "because he will not tell them his plans. He, in turn, is angry with them and with reason, for they are looking for a story and he is trying to make plans to capture Paris."[14]

Leclerc moved out early on Thursday, August 24. At 6:30 a.m. the Second Armored left Rambouillet in two tactical groups heading for Paris, with a third, as a decoy to distract the Germans, going through Versailles as Gerow had instructed. Leclerc was then supposed to head for the Eiffel Tower. As one historian has suggested, "This plan possibly reflected the very American idea that the Eiffel Tower is the center of Paris."[15] Leclerc, who had cleared his plan with de Gaulle, planned to enter Paris from the south. His first column, Tactical Group V under Colonel Pierre Billotte, would enter the city through the Porte d'Orléans; the second, Tactical Group T under Colonel Paul de Langlade, would enter through the Porte de Saint-Cloud. Once in Paris, the two would head for the Place de la Concorde, which was very close to von Choltitz's headquarters at the Hotel Meurice. The U.S. Fourth Infantry Division would continue to follow the French forces.

But the movement on August 24 quickly ran into trouble. Unlike on the 23rd, the French troops encountered heavy German resistance. This was attributable to the strategy Generals von Boineburg-Lengsfeld and von Choltitz had adopted of deploying most of the Paris garrison outside the city to cover the approaches. And to compound matters, where there was no German resistance the French population turned out in massive numbers to greet Leclerc's men, further delaying the advance. By late afternoon it was clear that the Second Armored was not going to get to Paris that day. Tactical Group V under Billotte had advanced thirteen miles, and by nightfall was still about five miles away from the Porte d'Orléans. Tactical Group T under de Langlade had crossed the Port de Sèvres, a wide highway bridge across the Seine, and by evening was two miles from the Porte de Saint-Cloud. But neither was going to push into Paris in the dark. And the battles that day had taken a toll. Seventy-one French soldiers had been killed, 225 wounded, and 21 were missing. Thirty-five tanks had been destroyed and more than 111 other vehicles had been lost.[16]

The Americans were perplexed at Leclerc's slow progress. Gerow complained to Bradley that Leclerc was "dancing to Paris" and "advancing on a one-tank front."[17] Bradley responded by ordering the U.S. Fourth Infantry Division to outflank the French and "slam it on to Paris" from the southeast. "To hell with prestige," he told his chief of staff, Colonel Lev Allen.[18]

Leclerc was equally upset. In the late afternoon he sent a Piper Cub to fly over the city and drop a note in the courtyard of the *préfecture de police. "Tenez bon. Nous arrivons."* Hang on. We're coming.[19]

All was not lost. Standing at a roadside junction not far from Trappes at about six-thirty, Leclerc saw a familiar face from North Africa leading his company of armored cars to a reserve position for the evening. "Dronne, what are you doing here?" he asked. Leclerc was addressing Captain Raymond Dronne, who had joined his forces in the Cameroons, fought across North Africa, and been wounded in Tunisia. Dronne was a combat commander Leclerc respected, and he wondered why he was heading away from the front lines. Dronne's troops had just successfully enveloped Fresnes.

"Mon general, I am returning to the axis of advance," Dronne replied, meaning he was returning to the main force of Colonel Billotte.[20]

Leclerc was surprised and decided to exercise his command authority. "Never carry out an idiotic order," he told Dronne. Leclerc believed there was no serious resistance east of Fresnes and that the roads to Paris were open. Gesticulating with his cane toward the capital, he told Dronne to move on to Paris immediately.

"At once, *mon general,*" Dronne replied. "But I have only two platoons and I am going to need more than that."

"Take what you can find and quickly," Leclerc replied. Dronne asked for further instructions. Was he to avoid German fortifications and head straight for the center of Paris?

"Correct," Leclerc replied. "Right into Paris, any way you like. Tell the Parisians and the Resistance not to lose courage and that tomorrow the whole division will be in Paris." In Dronne's retelling, Leclerc looked less tense and was now smiling. Paris would be entered today.[21]

Ironically, Dronne's company was made up primarily of Spanish Civil War veterans whose half-tracks were named for Spanish cities: *Madrid, Guadalajara, Brunete,* and *Guernica.* The men were Spaniards who had fought for the republic in Spain and were now engaged in another war against fascism. Before moving on Paris, Dronne felt he needed some armored support and asked a Lieutenant Michard, who commanded three tanks, to join him. He also picked up a platoon of engineers commanded by a Lieutenant Cancel, which brought his total force to 150 men, 3 Sherman tanks, 15 half-tracks, and a number of jeeps.

Dronne and his men moved out at 8 p.m. As they departed, a young man named Georges Chevallier stepped forward and offered to guide them through the tangled network of roads and streets leading to Paris. He understood how to go, and helped Dronne's force through the suburbs of L'Haÿ-les-Roses, Cachan, Arcueil, and Bicêtre. After forty-five minutes—and with no German contact—they were at the Porte d'Italie, an ancient gateway to Paris. Traveling along the same road that Napoléon had used when he returned from Elba, Dronne's troops were now in Paris. Parisians at first thought the incoming troops were Germans, but when they saw the American markings on the tanks and half-tracks they erupted in celebration. Dronne recognized that he had to push on, and miraculously found a young man on a moped who volunteered to lead the column to the center of Paris. A member of the Resistance, Lorenian Dikran, like Georges Chevallier, was calm and collected, and led Dronne to his objective, the Hôtel de Ville, or City Hall. Dronne chose the Hôtel de Ville because it symbolized the history of France and the rights and liberties of Frenchmen.

Led by Dikran, Dronne's force drove along the Avenue d'Italie, the Rue Baudricourt, the Rue Nationale, and the Rue Esquirol. They turned onto the Boulevard de l'Hôpital, crossed the Seine on the Pont d'Austerlitz, and then moved along the Seine on the Quai Henry IV and the Quai des Célestins to the center of the city and the Place d'Hôtel de Ville. The streets had been empty and no

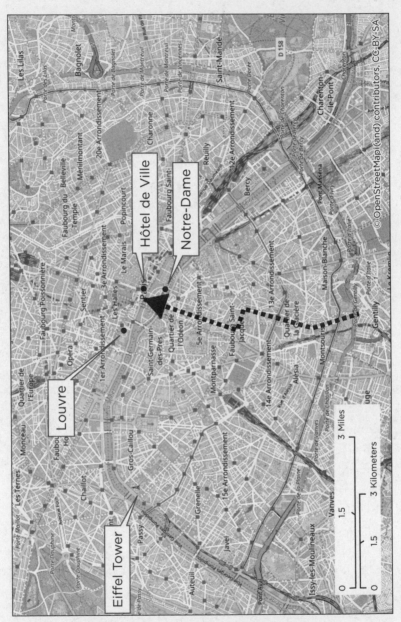

Figure 4: Captain Dronne's route into Paris

Captain Raymond Dronne, August 24, 1944

German troops interfered, although there was considerable gun-fire from other parts of the city.

It was 9:22 p.m. and Dronne entered the Hôtel de Ville. That was exactly 1,532 days, 3 hours, and 52 minutes since the first German troops had entered Paris in 1940.[22] Dronne was greeted at the door by men of the FFI, and cheered as he made his way up the main staircase to the grand salon. Just before Dronne arrived, Georges Bidault, the president of the National Resistance, had stood on a mess table in the refectory and announced that "the first tanks of the French Army have crossed the Seine and are in the heart of Paris."[23] As Bidault finished, the sound of tank treads moving toward the building could be heard. The men in the room sprang to their feet to sing the *Marseillaise*, and just as they finished, Dronne entered the building. They greeted him with an outpouring of affection. Standing before the crowd unshaven in his sweat-soaked uniform, Dronne also felt deeply moved.

Outside, on the Place d'Hôtel de Ville, crowds began to gather. As the men dismounted from their vehicles, they were warmly applauded by the Parisians. Pierre Crénesse, a reporter for French radio, saw the first soldier coming out of the lead tank and with his microphone open asked him where he was from. "Constantinople," replied Prilian Krikor. At the same time, the radioman in Dronne's company called back to Leclerc's headquarters, "We are at the Hôtel de Ville." [24]

Inside the Hôtel de Ville, Dronne was swept upstairs to the prefect's office, where he was officially welcomed by Bidault in the name of "soldiers without uniform" who had been fighting for France.[25] Crénesse was now in the building and spoke directly to the people of Paris by a telephone link to his studio:

> Tomorrow morning will be the dawn of a new day for the capital. Tomorrow morning Paris will be liberated, Paris will finally discover its true face. Four years of struggle, four years that have been, for many people, years of prison, years of pain, of torture and, for many more, a slow death in the Nazi concentration camps, but that's all over. . . . These soldiers of the Leclerc Division and their comrades in the FFI on the Place d'Hôtel de Ville, machine guns over their shoulders, automatic weapons in their arms, revolvers in their hands, renewing old acquaintances, seem to me to symbolize the resurrection of France, the union of fighting external armies and those of the Interior who have been hunting the Hun for the last five days and who have already liberated the main public buildings of the city.[26]

He then handed the phone to Bidault, who spoke briefly, emphasizing that Germany was not beaten and urging all Frenchmen to support the Allies. Colonel Rol, who had just arrived at the

Hôtel de Ville, then spoke, noting that Paris had been largely liberated thanks to the guerrilla tactics carried out by the FFI.

> Open the radio to Paris for the Allied armies, hunt down and destroy the remnants of German divisions, link up with the Leclerc Division in a common victory—that is the mission that is being accomplished by the FFI of the Ile-de-France and of Paris, simmering with a sacred hatred and patriotism.[27]

As they were speaking, the great fourteen-ton bell in the south tower of Notre-Dame began to ring. It had not been rung since June 1940, when the occupation began. Charles Luizet, the prefect of police, had sent a dozen policemen to the cathedral to ring the bell. It was quickly answered by the even greater nineteen-ton bell in the Church of the Sacré-Cœur, dominating the city's skyline in Montmartre. Over the radio, all the churches were urged to begin ringing their bells—which they did. All over Paris, the ringing of the church bells—which had not occurred in four years—signaled that the occupation was over.

Throughout Paris the celebration began. All over the city people threw open their windows to listen to the bells and rejoice at the victory. Others rushed into the streets singing the *Marseillaise*, banging pots and waving French flags. It was a celebration long in the making and deeply appreciated.

As the celebration began, two policemen arrived at the Hôtel de Ville to escort Captain Dronne to see Luizet, Chaban-Delmas, and Parodi at the *préfecture*. These were the Gaullist leaders in Paris, and they wanted to emphasize their presence and underline the government they represented. When Dronne arrived, Parodi spoke to the radio audience: "I have in front of me a French captain who is the first to arrive in Paris. His face is red, he is grubby, and he needs a shave, and yet I want to embrace him." After another public reception Luizet asked Dronne if there was anything he needed. "A bath," said Dronne.[28] He was taken to the rather luxurious bathroom in Luizet's private quarters, where he bathed and freshened up. But there was no time to waste at the *préfecture*. He took his leave and returned to his men at the Hôtel de Ville. With the celebrations going on at full intensity, Dronne spread his sleeping bag in the street and went to sleep. Leclerc's men had made it to Paris. It was a remarkable accomplishment.

Dronne's company was not the only French unit to arrive in Paris that evening. Colonel Paul de Langlade's force, led by Lieutenant Colonel Jacques Massu, had crossed the Pont de Sèvres

Lieutenant Colonel Jacques Massu

into the city.* But de Langlade had ordered Massu to hold up. "That is not your mission," he said, speaking of the liberation of Paris.[29] For de Langlade the liberation had personal aspects. He picked up a telephone and called his mother, who lived in the city. It was the first time in almost five years they had spoken. He told her he would be with her the next afternoon and that she should stay inside until then.

The arrival of French forces in Paris did not mean that Paris was liberated. But it was a major achievement, and perhaps no one was more pleased by it than General von Choltitz.

---

* Jacques Massu became a very successful and sometimes controversial military commander after World War II. In 1957 he became military governor of Algiers and suppressed the FLN, sometimes with tactics that exceeded the permissible. Massu became a hero to the Europeans in Algeria but a villain to the left in France and the Algerian nationalists. In 1958, when anti-government riots broke out in France, he led the movement to recall de Gaulle to power and became a strong supporter of the Fifth Republic. When four generals in Algeria launched a coup in 1961, he stood by de Gaulle and helped quash the coup. De Gaulle made him military governor of Metz, and in 1966 promoted Massu to the five-star rank of general of the army and made him commander of the French army in Germany. In 1968, when students and workers were demonstrating against the government, Massu convinced de Gaulle to remain in office, and de Gaulle did so. Massu retired the following year, and died in 2002 at the age of 94. In later life he expressed regrets at his methods in Algeria and said, "We could have done things differently." *Times of London*, October 29, 2002.

— VIII —

A Field of Ruins

"Paris must not fall into enemy hands except as a field of ruins."

—ADOLF HITLER, AUGUST 23, 1944

On August 23, the day after von Choltitz dispatched Rolf Nordling to contact the Allies, Hitler sent a message to Field Marshal Walther Model and von Choltitz demanding that Paris be held at all costs, and that if it could not be held it should be turned into a field of ruins. Said Hitler:

> The defense of Paris is of decisive military and political significance. Its loss would tear open the whole coastal front north of the Seine and deprive Germany of bases for very long-range warfare against England.
>
> Historically, the loss of Paris always meant the loss of France. The Führer repeats his order that Paris has to be defended. . . . The strongest measures to quell insurrection inside the city must be taken. . . . The bridges across the Seine are to be prepared for demolition. Paris must not fall into enemy hands except as a field of ruins.[1]

Von Choltitz was stunned by the message. And he was also ashamed. "Four days ago the factual order might have been considered. But the situation had changed. The enemy was moving rapidly toward Paris. He had captured the bridge at Melun. We had no troops available. The First [German] Army consisted of a few remaining troops and was no fighting force worth mentioning. I had no troops to confront tank divisions."[2] Von Choltitz believed the order had no military validity and despaired at the outright hatred it contained. After reading it, he showed it to his second in command, Colonel Hans Jay, an old friend. They were standing on the balcony outside von Choltitz's office in the Hotel Meurice on the Rue de Rivoli. As Jay recalled, "In front of us the Tuileries lay in sunshine. To our right was the Place de la Concorde and to our left the Louvre. The scene merely underlined the madness of the medieval command."[3] Von Choltitz put the order in his pocket and showed it to no one else.

Later that day he called another old friend, Lieutenant General Hans Speidel, the chief of staff at Field Marshal Model's headquarters in Cambrai. Von Choltitz and Speidel were friends from the prewar army and the Russian front, and von Choltitz considered Speidel very efficient and humane.* "Thank you for the beautiful order," said von Choltitz.

"What order, General?"

"The Field of Ruins Order." Von Choltitz then went on to tell

---

* General Hans Speidel, who was chief of staff to Rommel, Kluge, and Model, remained in his position only for another week. He was then arrested for his role in the July 20 plot. An Army Court of Honor consisting of Field Marshal von Rundstedt, General Heinz Guderian, and Field Marshal Wilhelm Keitel ruled that he should not be expelled from the German Army but tried by court-martial. He remained in army captivity until the end of the war, when he was released by the French. In postwar Germany, Speidel played an important role as military adviser to Chancellor Konrad Adenauer, was instrumental in the creation of the Bundeswehr, and as a four-star general (the first in the Bundeswehr) oversaw the integration of the Bundeswehr into NATO. He was appointed supreme commander of NATO Ground Forces in 1957 and held that position until his retirement in September 1963.

Speidel what he had done. Three tons of dynamite in Notre-Dame, two tons in the Dome at Les Invalides, and one ton in the Chamber of Deputies. He said he was presently working to detonate the Arc de Triomphe to improve visibility. "Hopefully you agree, Speidel."

"Yes, yes, General."

"Yes, but you ordered it."

"We did not order it. The Führer ordered it."

"Excuse me," von Choltitz replied. "You have passed on the order and you will be responsible to history. I'll tell you what else I've ordered. The Madeleine and the Opera are taken together. And the Eiffel Tower. I'll detonate it so its metal structure will lie in front of the destroyed bridges."

Speidel finally realized that von Choltitz was not serious and that he was talking just to illustrate the craziness of the order. He

General Hans Speidel

replied, "Oh, General, we are thankful you are in Paris." They remained on the phone together for several more minutes, but then silence prevailed. "We knew," said von Choltitz later. "We are at home in similar intellectual realms. On the telephone one better not talk about orders you disagree with. Important that we do not discuss the factual content of the order. Speidel knew like myself that it all did not matter anymore and what was left was embarrassment and empty words."[4]

Von Choltitz learned later that Model's headquarters had received the order from Hitler but did not pass it on. His staff had found it on the network and given it to him.[5] Some Germans in France agreed with von Choltitz and Speidel that Paris should not become a field of ruins. The same afternoon that he spoke to Speidel, von Choltitz received a phone call from *Generaloberst* Otto Dessloch, the commander of Luftflotte 3, the German tactical air force in France.

"Herr General," said Dessloch, "I have orders to discuss with you about the air attack on Paris."

Von Choltitz was shocked. Was the Luftwaffe going to bomb Paris while it was still occupied? Von Choltitz answered carefully. "I completely agree, but I hope you will come during the day."

"No, we cannot risk that," said Dessloch.

"You mean you are going to ignite the city with your ninety bombers at night? How do you think to do that?"

"We have been ordered to discuss that with you. You are supposed to name the targets."

"Can you guarantee that you will hit the targets that I name at night?" von Choltitz responded.

Dessloch said that they would hit areas of the city, but he could not guarantee they could hit precise targets.

"Yes, do this," von Choltitz replied. "But one thing is clear. I'll withdraw my troops. You cannot assume that I'll allow myself to be burned together with my soldiers by you. You probably know

I've been ordered to stay in Paris. You'll be responsible for my leaving the city."

There was a lengthy pause in the conversation. Then Dessloch replied, "Yes, that probably means it cannot be done."

"I'm thinking that as well," von Choltitz replied.[6] Later he wrote that it was obvious that he and Dessloch agreed and "did not wish this senseless and barbaric bombardment of the city." But with their phone conversation likely monitored by the Gestapo, they had to talk to each other "tongue in cheek" so that everything would seem to be in line with orders.[7]

August 23 and 24 were difficult days for von Choltitz. He was determined to preserve Paris, but had to do so in such a way that he would not be relieved of command. He was aided by Ambassador Otto Abetz, who called on him to say that he was leaving Paris. Von Choltitz and Abetz found themselves in agreement on how to handle Paris, and with the end in sight, Abetz asked, "General, how can I be of help?"

"Mr. Ambassador, how can you possibly help me?"

"General, I will send a cable to headquarters and to Ribbentrop in which I complain about your brutal behavior in Paris."

Von Choltitz was overwhelmed. He and Abetz had met a number of times before, and he could not believe what Abetz was saying. He jumped up from his desk and put his hands on Abetz's shoulders. "You really want to do this? Then you are one of us."

"Yes," Abetz replied. "That I will do."

As von Choltitz noted later, the cable Abetz sent to Berlin "protected me from being recalled or eliminated in a way that was typical for the time."[8]

In Paris itself, the situation was tense. On the morning of the 23rd, a German armored unit not part of von Choltitz's command was taking advantage of the truce and moving through the city to the east. As it reached the foot of the Champs-Élysées, near the

Grand Palais, it was fired on by Paris police, with one soldier being killed. The Germans responded immediately. The Grand Palais was a major Paris landmark between the Seine and the Champs-Élysées. It was one of the largest buildings in Paris, and the site of major expositions since the Universal Exhibition of 1900. It also housed the police of the 8th Arrondissement in the basement. The German column was determined to avenge the shooting. They launched two small unmanned "Goliath" tanks—four feet long, two feet wide, and one foot high, carrying fifty kilograms of explosives, essentially remote-controlled bombs—at the Grand Palais. When they exploded, the explosions were so great that buildings shook for blocks around and the sound of the explosions echoed across Paris. There was a Swedish circus under way at the Palais, and the lions, tigers, and horses bolted for freedom, as did a collection of prostitutes imprisoned in the Palais by the police. With animals stampeding and the Germans shooting at will, the situation deteriorated quickly. At noon order was restored when forty Paris policemen surrendered under a white flag. They were delivered to von Choltitz, who said he would treat them as prisoners of war. Firemen finally extinguished the blaze, but the Grand Palais was left as a shell, with its interior totally destroyed. The episode demonstrated German strength and served to put the Resistance on notice.[9]

Later on the 23rd von Choltitz was startled when his chief of staff, Colonel Friedrich von Unger, told him that a lieutenant colonel from their military police had come in and suggested that since Paris could not be held, von Choltitz should order a retreat. Von Choltitz saw the officer immediately and raked him over the coals. "I reminded him that he had to follow orders, and that I wished no critique of the situation. Imagine what would have happened if we avoided a decision in this moment. The last bit of a soldier's honor would have been lost."[10]

Von Choltitz ordered Unger to immediately assemble all head-quarters officers. When they were together, he spoke forcefully. "Gentlemen, I have made the acquaintance of a rebellious officer for the first time in my life. He wanted to tell his commanding general to give orders he does not approve. I have been sent here by the Führer, and I alone am responsible. We'll do exactly what I order. He who refuses I will force into obedience with a weapon. Everyone take their places and wait for orders. Should I die, and this is an order, Colonel Jay will take my place and the chief of staff, Colonel von Unger, will assist him."

Von Choltitz said later he had to ask for obedience from those under him because he was better suited to understand the situation and because he carried the responsibility. "Don't think this game in Paris was easy for me. Circumstances had forced a role on me I really was not suited for. Often my instinct spoke against me, and I felt muddied. Often when I was alone in my room I thought of the clear relationships I had among soldiers and I said to myself: God, how repugnant all of this is."[11]

The situation in Paris was indeed unraveling. The Resistance was pushing ahead, and von Choltitz did not want to engage in street battles. So he decided to issue a public statement that he hoped Parisians would respect. Using a Luftwaffe airplane, he dropped thousands of leaflets over the city.

FRENCHMEN!

Paris is still in the hands of the Germans! . . . Under our protection it has known four years of relative peace. For us it continues to be one of the beautiful cities of the Europe for which we have fought, we should prefer to preserve it against the dangers that threaten it.

BUT SHOOTING CONTINUES IN PARIS.

Criminal elements insist on terrorizing the city! Blood has been spilled, French blood as well as German! . . . The extent of these riots is as yet small, yet it is approaching the limits compatible with the humanitarian feelings of the German troops in Paris.

It will not be difficult to make a brutal ending to all this! It would be a simple matter to leave Paris after first blowing up all warehouses, all factories, bridges, and railway stations, and to seal the suburbs hermetically off if the city should be encircled. Considering the shortage of food supplies, water, and electricity, this would mean a terrible catastrophe in less than 24 hours!

. . . . You may rely on the humanitarian sentiments of the German troops, who will not act unless driven to the end of their patience. You may rely on our love for this marvelous center of European culture, on our sympathy for all reasonable Frenchmen, for the women and children of Paris, but if all these things are not considered sacred by the populace itself, there would no longer be any reason for us to remain tolerant.

We demand the immediate and unconditional cessation of acts of violence against us and against citizens. We demand that the citizens of Paris defend themselves against the terrorists; that they maintain in themselves their right to order and calm, and that they go about their daily work in a peaceable manner.

This, and this alone, can guarantee the life of the city, its victualment, and its salvation.

COMMANDANT OF THE WEHRMACHT
OF GREATER PARIS.[12]

The combination of the incident at the Grand Palais and von Choltitz's public appeal helped subdue the violence. The Allies were coming and the Resistance was also running out of ammunition. Figures compiled by the Paris police indicate that in the first four days of the revolt the police had lost sixty-two men and the German Army sixty-eight. Most of those losses occurred before the truce Nordling arranged. The bulk of the casualties were in the Resistance, where 483 had been killed and nearly 1,200 wounded. Most of the fighting had taken place in working-class neighborhoods. In the fashionable 16th Arrondissement no one had been wounded and no one killed.[13] This made the Resistance look a bit like a civil war.

Another problem was the growing food shortage. Again it was rich versus poor. In the fashionable parts of Paris food was always available, at exorbitant prices. In poorer sections there was almost none. In addition, the city's gas had been turned off, and electricity was available only a few hours each day. The lack of electricity affected the city's water supply as pumping stations needed power. All of this meant the desire for the liberation knew no bounds. The Paris police were instructed to put their uniforms back on and to be prepared to defend "republican institutions."[14]

Said differently, as the Allies approached, the mood in Paris changed significantly. The Resistance newspaper *Combat* captured the mood when it wrote, "The Paris that is fighting this evening wants to command tomorrow. Not for the sake of power, but for justice; not for the sake of politics, but for morality; not for the sake of dominating the country, but for its greatness."[15] By contrast, the Communist newspaper *L'Humanité* kept up the appeal for violence. "Attack is the best form of defense. Harass the enemy. Not a single Hun should leave insurgent Paris alive."[16]

Late that evening, von Choltitz had a lengthy telephone conversation with Model's headquarters. Speaking to General

Günther Blumentritt, who had been chief of staff to Rundstedt and was now Model's operations officer, he explained that the situation in Paris had begun to spin out of control, and because of the barricades that had been constructed, it was impossible to move supplies to various German strongpoints throughout the city. "There is shooting everywhere," said von Choltitz. He was vastly exaggerating—most of the city was absolutely quiet—but he continued: "The shootings and other retaliatory actions called for by the Führer can no longer be implemented. In order to blow up bridges, we need to battle our way to them; in the case of 75 bridges, this is no longer possible. Any such measure could drive the majority of the still passive population into the hands of the enemy." [17] Von Choltitz was covering his back by lying. But he wanted this information on the record.

Field Marshal Model was not surprised by von Choltitz's position. He too knew that Paris was not defensible, and that if he were going to halt the Allied advance, surrendering Paris was a useful first step. Later that night he spoke to Alfred Jodl, chief of operations at Hitler's headquarters. Jodl told Model that the Führer was enraged that Paris might be lost, and he wanted it held at all costs. If the Wehrmacht "could not crush the despicable rabble" on the streets of Paris, it would "cover itself with the worst shame and dishonor in its history." Model was unimpressed. He had already decided to form a new defensive line on the Marne and the Somme east of Paris. "Tell the Führer that I know what I am doing," he once again told a speechless Jodl.[18] Model knew that to defend Paris would be to destroy Army Group B's ability to regroup and halt the Allied advance. That, he believed, was more important. He did not intend to overturn von Choltitz's approach.

That same evening von Choltitz placed a call to his wife in Baden-Baden. Unfortunately, she was out at the famous opera house there watching a performance of Wagner's *Flying Dutchman*.

Notified that she had a telephone call, she left the performance and hurried home, only to find that her husband not had been able to hold the line open. He left a message. "We are doing our duty." That was it. She would not see her husband again until November 1947, when he was released from American captivity.*[19]

Finally, on the night of August 23, another conversation took place that was vital for the surrender of Paris. Meeting at the Swedish consulate were Emil Bender, the Abwehr (military intelligence) agent who often worked with von Choltitz, and Lorraine Cruse, aide to General Jacques Chaban-Delmas, the Gaullist military chief in Paris. The meeting had been organized by Raoul Nordling, and it was important for arranging Paris's surrender. "General von Choltitz cannot capitulate without an exchange of fire," Bender told Cruse. "His family is threatened; they are hostages to Hitler. He is a soldier bound by the requirements of military honor. He simply cannot surrender without a fight. So it is necessary for you to fight. But why attack on all sides? The key to Paris's defense is the Hotel Meurice where the general is based. . . . The General will defend himself. . . . [but] once he is defeated, all other points of resistance will collapse."[20] The message could not have been clearer. Von Choltitz would not surrender to the Resistance, but he would to the French army. Leclerc had to get his forces to the Meurice as soon as possible. Cruse immediately returned to Chaban-Delmas and passed the word. Chaban-Delmas in turn immediately notified Leclerc.

August 24 dawned overcast, and in Paris it was relatively quiet. The Resistance was low on ammunition and the Germans were staying off the streets. The principal fighting took place to the

---

* Von Choltitz was originally placed in captivity with other German generals at Trent Park in England. When the war ended, they were transferred to Clinton, Mississippi, where they remained until released in 1947.

south and west of the city. Like his predecessor, General Hans von Boineburg-Lengsfeld, von Choltitz had deployed the bulk of his garrison, roughly fifteen thousand men, to guard the approaches to Paris from the south and west. These forces were under the command of Major General Hubertus von Aulock, and von Choltitz warned them to be ready. The German troops under Aulock were a mixed bag. There were a few combat veterans, but it was mostly young soldiers, sixteen and seventeen, who had been assigned to man the anti-aircraft guns in Paris, and many who were just part of the occupation. Aulock had no field artillery, very few tanks, and a lot of anti-aircraft guns hopelessly out of place in a land battle. Nevertheless, his troops did surprisingly well that day, preventing the French—with the exception of Dronne—from entering Paris. Later that afternoon Aulock told von Choltitz he was abandoning his position and moving east to join Model. Von Choltitz briefly considered whether to order Aulock to join the forces in Paris, but decided it wasn't worth it. The troops were young and inexperienced, and there was no need to lose their heavy equipment.[21]

Also on the afternoon of the 24th, von Choltitz received a telephone call from Leclerc's headquarters. Would he consider an exchange of letters in which he would surrender Paris? Von Choltitz declined. "Before the end of hostilities I do not exchange letters with the generals of the enemy."[22] It seems clear that von Choltitz knew that the only way he could save his family in Baden-Baden from Hitler's *Sippenhaft* was to go down fighting.

Another problem von Choltitz confronted was the fate of German female office workers in France. As defeat became evident, von Choltitz had facilitated the transfer of some thirty thousand female army workers back to Germany. But on August 24, some sixty remained, mostly support staff in his headquarters. Von Choltitz asked Nordling to protect them. It was arranged that they would all be taken on the morning of the 25th to the Hotel Bristol and placed under the protection of the Red Cross. Unfortunately, it didn't work out, and instead of being protected they fell into French hands and remained in captivity for almost a year.[23]

Whether Hitler ever asked "Is Paris burning?" (*"Brennt Paris?"*) remains a matter of historical dispute. In his memoirs, von Choltitz says he never saw the question, but was told about it later.[24] The English historian Matthew Cobb devotes considerable space to the question and concludes that Hitler did not say it.[25] But Larry Collins and Dominique Lapierre in their bestseller *Is Paris Burning?* insist that he did, and devote several pages to illustrating how Hitler asked Jodl, "Jodl! *Brennt Paris?*"[26] It really doesn't matter. Hitler's August 23 order that Paris should become a field of ruins was sufficient. And von Choltitz did his best to avoid it.

But he had to conceal his intent. Twice on August 24, von Choltitz was on the phone with Günther Blumentritt at Model's headquarters. He wanted to give the impression of continuous activity to halt the Allied advance, when in reality he was doing nothing. All of his soldiers were in action, he told Blumentritt, when that was far from the case. He also told Blumentritt that regardless of the Allied advance, he was staying in Paris. "I want to emphasize how serious the situation in Paris becomes with every passing hour. . . . I will use the remaining strength of Aulock's forces to push east to make contact with German troops and above all to receive instruction on how to fight on."[27] The replies from Berlin were what von Choltitz had expected. He was ordered to defend Paris to the last man.

On the evening of August 24, with Allied forces approaching, von Choltitz hosted a farewell dinner at the Meurice for his staff. They were in a private dining room overlooking the Rue de Rivoli, the dress was formal, and the niceties were all in place. Von Choltitz was joined by his deputy Hans Jay; his chief of staff Friedrich von Unger; his aide Dankwart von Arnim; two ordnance officers;

and his two secretaries Cita Krebben and Hildegarde Grün. The food was superb and the champagne was plentiful. The principal item of conversation was the Saint Bartholomew's Day massacre—the massacre of French Protestants—which had occurred in Paris on August 24, 1572, exactly 372 years earlier.

Von Choltitz was also plunged in thought. "I had the heavy feeling that our ancestors did not have to face such conflicts and did not face such isolation. I knew my own wife and children were threatened by a regime that could deprive them of their freedom or take their lives. On the other side there were hundreds of thousands of women and children to be protected. The seriousness of the hour was immense."[28]

Suddenly the bells of Paris began to ring. They had not rung for four years. The sound was breathtaking. Cita Krebben turned to von Choltitz and asked why the bells were ringing. "What does that mean?"

"They are ringing because the Allies have arrived in Paris," von Choltitz said. "Why else do you suppose they would be ringing?"

Von Choltitz's officers seemed shocked. He steadied them. "What else did you expect? You've been sitting here in your own dream world for four years. What do you know about this war? You've seen nothing but your own pleasant life in Paris. You haven't seen what's happened to Germany in Russia and Normandy. Gentlemen, Germany has lost this war, and we have lost it with her."[29]

The dinner broke up. Von Choltitz returned to his office and placed a call to Army Group B. Unger, who checked with the staff outside, confirmed that a vanguard of the Allies had arrived in the city and that the main body would come in the morning. Speidel soon answered the phone at Model's headquarters.

"Good evening, Speidel," said von Choltitz. He then took the phone out onto his balcony, where the sound of the bells was loudest. "Do you hear that?"

"Yes, I hear bells ringing," said Speidel.

"Correct. The American-French army is moving into the city."

After a long pause, von Choltitz asked Speidel for orders. Speidel declined. "You know I am not allowed to give orders." Von Choltitz then asked to speak with Field Marshal Model. Model had been on a phone extension listening to the conversation but shook his head. He did not wish to speak to von Choltitz. Speidel then said that Model had no orders to give.

"Well then, dear Speidel, I can only say adieu. Look after my wife in Baden-Baden and protect her and the children."

"Yes, we will do that. We promise, General." [30]

So ended the German occupation of Paris. Von Choltitz would surrender to Leclerc the next day. Against all odds he had kept Paris intact. It was not the field of ruins Hitler had ordered. Field Marshal Walther Model also deserves some credit. From the time of his arrival from the Russian front to succeed Kluge, he knew that Paris could not be defended and so he concentrated on regrouping German armies to the east. He did not encourage von Choltitz, but he knew what von Choltitz was doing and allowed him to do so.

Before von Choltitz went to bed that evening, he received a visit from the young officer he had met before the war on the Mulde—the officer sent by Berlin to destroy Paris's bridges, Captain Werner Ebernach. Like von Choltitz, Ebernach had heard the bells and understood their meaning. He did not wish to go into an Allied prison as a POW, or to take his men with him. He told von Choltitz his job was over, the bridges had been prepared for destruction, and did von Choltitz have any more assignments for him?

"No, Ebernach, I have no further orders for you," said von Choltitz.

Ebernach then asked if his unit, which was part of the First German Army, could withdraw. He told von Choltitz he would leave behind a section of men to detonate the charges they had planted in the bridges.

Von Choltitz was moved. "*Ja*, Ebernach," he replied. "Take all your men and leave us."[31] It was a gift from Heaven. Without Ebernach's men, Paris's bridges could not be destroyed. Von Choltitz went to his room and went fast to sleep. Three hours later, the men of the 813th *Pionierkompanie* left Paris, crossing the bridges they had been sent to destroy.

Day of Liberation

"One of the great days of all time."
—ERNIE PYLE, AUGUST 25, 1944

F riday, August 25, was a perfect day. Not a cloud in the sky. Ironically, it was also the day of the Feast of Saint Louis, honoring the patron saint of France. Nothing could have been more appropriate. The German troops, under General Hubertus von Aulock, defending the approaches to Paris had retreated to join Field Marshal Model's main force east of the city, and the historic gates were open. General Dietrich von Choltitz had deployed the remaining German forces—some fifteen thousand men—at strongpoints throughout the city, but not in the streets. They were to hold their position, but not attack. That meant that General Leclerc's Second Armored Division and the U.S. Fourth Infantry Division could enter the city without a fight. As they did, they were welcomed by more than a million Parisians, as well dressed as they could manage after four years of occupation, and laden with wine and food for the celebration.

The incoming troops initially headed directly toward the center of Paris. Colonel de Langlade's forces moved into the city across the Pont de Sèvres and toward the Place de l'Étoile and down the Champs-Élysées. Colonel Billotte's came through the southern Porte d'Italie toward the *préfecture*, just as Dronne had done the night before. The U.S. Fourth Infantry Division also came in through the Porte d'Italie but turned east at the Bastille heading for Vincennes and the eastern suburbs in pursuit of the retreating Germans. Leclerc entered the city about 7:45 a.m., met up with Chaban-Delmas at a restaurant, and proceeded to the *préfecture*. Later they would go to the Gare Montparnasse, which de Gaulle had told Leclerc would be their headquarters.

Hitler was at it again early that morning, ordering that Paris be defended to the end, including its destruction as a final gesture. "The parts of the city that are in revolt must be destroyed."[1] Jodl sent the order to Model, who passed it along (without comment) to von Choltitz. Later that morning von Choltitz replied. He was covering his tracks. "I have ordered the bridges across the Seine on the eastern side of the city blown up, but destruction of the bridges in the city centre proved impossible because our own troops were south of the river. Our situation remains unchanged. Paris is burning in multiple locations. The enemy is attacking our positions with tanks. I have been asked to capitulate three times, and I have refused it each time."[2] The fact was no bridges in Paris had been destroyed, the city was not on fire, and the Allies were thus far avoiding the German strongpoints. Von Choltitz had indeed been asked to surrender three times: by Leclerc yesterday and again this morning, as well as another effort by Nordling and the Resistance. Each time von Choltitz refused, wanting to be involved in hostilities first.

The mood in Paris that morning was unprecedented. As one GI said, "Fifteen solid miles of cheering, deliriously happy people waiting to shake your hand, to kiss you, to shower you with food and wine." The military historian S. L. A. Marshall later acknowledged that sixty-seven bottles of champagne had been given to him that day.[3] Jeeps and tanks were soon covered with flowers. They also soon became covered with what Thomas Wolf, a reporter for the Fourth Infantry Division, called "the most beautiful girls I had ever seen."[4] It was a love match like the world had never seen.

But reality dawned quickly. The German strongpoints had to be neutralized. As Leclerc's men moved toward the center of the city, the strongpoints loomed menacingly ahead. The most serious were the Palais du Luxembourg and the Prince Eugene barracks on the Place de la République. The Palais du Luxembourg, which was the prewar home of the French Senate, had been the headquarters of the Luftwaffe in France and was now the home of the Waffen SS. The SS, unlike the German military, were determined to fight to the end, and the possibility that they would destroy the Palais could not be ruled out. The Prince Eugene barracks on the Place de la République had been built by Napoléon III and

Parisians welcome troops liberating Paris

could house more than three thousand troops. It was constructed like a fortress and was virtually impossible to penetrate. Other strongpoints included the École Militaire near the Eiffel Tower; the National Assembly on the Quai d'Orsay just across the Seine from the Meurice; the *Kommandantur* on the Place de l'Opéra; the Hôtel Majestic near the Arc de Triomphe, which had been the German army headquarters in France; and the Hôtel Crillon and the Navy Ministry on the Place de la Concorde. Both the Crillon and the Navy Ministry helped protect von Choltitz's headquarters in the Meurice. The Germans were defending the center of Paris, and would have to be defeated.

It soon became clear that the best approach was to attack and capture von Choltitz and get him to order the surrender. The fighting on the Rue de Rivoli began about 1 p.m. Colonel Billotte divided his attacking force into two columns under the command of Lieutenant Colonel Jean de la Horie. The first, a tank company under Captain Jacques Branet, moved up the Rue de Rivoli. The second, an infantry company under Lieutenant Henri Karcher, moved under the arcade on the north side of the street. Meanwhile in the Meurice, von Choltitz and his staff were having lunch as usual. With shooting outside, Colonel Jay urged von Choltitz not to take his regular seat with his back to the window. "No," said von Choltitz, "today of all days, I take my regular place."[5]

Gradually the French troops worked their way up the Rue de Rivoli to the Meurice. At 1:50, Corporal Helmut Mayer, von Choltitz's orderly, walked discreetly over to von Choltitz and whispered in his ear—"*Sie kommen, Herr General.*" Von Choltitz finished his meal and then rose to address his staff. "Gentlemen, our last combat has begun. May God protect you all. And I hope the survivors fall into the hands of regular troops, and not those of the population."[6] With that he walked slowly out of the room. Below on the street the fighting was getting intense. The German defenders were holding firm, and the French tanks began their barrage. Back in his office, von Choltitz began a letter to Nordling thanking him for his efforts. At the same time a French tank turned its gun on the entrance to the hotel. "My God, what's he going to do?" asked von Choltitz's aide, Dankvort von Arnim. "He's going to use it," said von Choltitz. "There will be a little noise, and we'll be in trouble."[7]

Von Choltitz also had made a decision. A few moments earlier his old friend Colonel Jay had told him he must make up his mind. "Are you going to sit here and play hide-and-seek with the Americans all day or are you going to surrender and get this damn business over with?"[8] Now he had decided. He disliked causing his men to die in a hopeless cause. Von Choltitz called his chief of staff Friedrich von Unger to inform him. If the FFI were taking the Meurice, they would continue the fight, he said, but if regular troops came in, the building commander was to surrender after a few shots had been fired. He also told Unger to take down the flag when the Allies entered the building.

Shortly after 2 p.m. the French forces made their way to the entrance of the Meurice. Lieutenant Karcher and his troops entered the building, and after a brief exchange of gunfire, the German commander ordered his men to cease firing. They raised their hands and became prisoners. "Where is your general?" asked Karcher.[9] The way to von Choltitz's office was pointed out, and Karcher moved on it.

Von Choltitz waited for the French in a small room upstairs, along with his principal staff officers. They were all seated at a long table with their pistols in front of them on the table. Corporal Mayer again announced their arrival. "*Sie kommen, Herr General.*" They were led by Lieutenant Karcher. When they entered the room, Karcher asked, "*Sprecken sie Deutsch?*" ("Do you speak German?") "Probably better than you do," von Choltitz replied.[10]

At that moment, Colonel Jean de la Horie came in and took

charge. De la Horie saluted von Choltitz and asked, "General, are you ready to surrender?" Von Choltitz, returning the salute, said, "Yes, I'm ready."[11] Colonel de la Horie then told von Choltitz to follow him. He would take him to General Leclerc. They went down a back staircase at the Meurice to von Choltitz's car but could not find the keys. Then they walked up from the cellar to the Rue Castiglione. Once in the street they were surrounded by Parisians who vented their hatred at von Choltitz. They turned onto the Rue de Rivoli, toward the French command's armored vehicles, and the crowd became even more antagonistic. One of von Choltitz's aides, Dr. Otto Kayser, who in peacetime was a professor of literature at the University of Cologne, was shot in the head and died instantly. Men shouted and women continued to spit on von Choltitz. Finally, a French Red Cross woman in uniform approached and walked next to von Choltitz as they made their way to the half-track that would take them to Leclerc's headquarters at the *préfecture*. With her body she shielded von Choltitz from the crowd. When they reached the half-track for their journey to Leclerc, von Choltitz embraced the woman who had shielded him. "*Madame, comme Jeanne d'Arc,*" he said.[12]

The journey to the *préfecture* was without incident. When he arrived, von Choltitz found himself guarded by the Paris police. He was escorted downstairs to the billiard room where Leclerc was waiting, along with Chaban-Delmas and Major General Raymond Barton, commander of the U.S. Fourth Infantry Division. As von Choltitz remembered, "A general stepped toward me, wellmannered, and with perfect soldierly demeanor said, 'I am General Leclerc. You must be General von Choltitz. Why did you not accept my letter?'" Leclerc spoke in French. Von Choltitz answered in German. "I will not accept letters before the fight is over."[13] With the preliminaries dispensed with, Leclerc and von Choltitz sat down to go over the surrender document that the French had prepared paragraph by paragraph. The document contained reference to the strongpoints still fighting, and von Choltitz agreed to surrender them. "I accepted the responsibility for the end of hostilities and wanted to do this with a full conscience. My opinion was that a general when he sees the fight is hopeless does not sacrifice his men unnecessarily. I did not want the bases that were spread throughout the city to continue the fight after their leaders had surrendered."[14]

THE PROVISIONAL GOVERNMENT OF THE FRENCH REPUBLIC

Act of Surrender concluded between the Divisional General Leclerc, commanding the French Forces of Paris and General von Choltitz, Military Commander of the German Forces in the Paris Region.

Generals von Choltitz, Leclerc, and Barton

All the articles here below apply to the units of the Wehr-macht throughout the command of General von Choltitz.

(1) Immediate orders will be issued to the commanders of the strong-points to cease fire and fly the white flag: arms will be collected and troops will be mustered without arms in the open, there to await orders. The arms will be intact.

(2) The order of battle, including mobile units and de-pots of materials throughout the command, will be handed over. The depots will be handed over intact with their books.

(3) A list of the destruction to works and depots.

(4) As many German staff officers as there are strong-points or garrisons will be sent to General Leclerc's head-quarters.

(5) The conditions in which the personnel of the Weh-rmacht will be evacuated will be arranged by General Le-clerc's staff.

(6) Once these articles have been signed and the orders transmitted, members of the Wehrmacht who continue to fight will no longer enjoy the protection of the laws of war.

Paris, 25 August 1944.

Von Choltitz questioned paragraph six. He told Leclerc that there might be some German toops passing through Paris on their way east who were not subject to his command and therefore not subject to the Act of Surrender. Leclerc understood. He added a sentence to paragraph six to remedy the problem: "Nevertheless, the case of any German soldiers in or crossing Paris who are not under the General's command will be fairly examined."[15]

The meeting continued without hostility. Suddenly, Colonel Rol and his deputy Maurice Kriegel-Valrimont, who led the FFI in Paris, appeared and wanted to be included. Leclerc originally re-

*General von Choltitz signing the surrender
document in Paris, August 25, 1944*

sisted, maintaining that a surrender document was only between soldiers, but Rol insisted. The surrender document must include the FFI, he said, and no cease-fire would be valid without his agreement. Charles Luizet, the Gaullist who was now heading the police department, convinced Leclerc to include Colonel Rol so the shooting could stop. Whatever political differences there were could be resolved later. Leclerc agreed and permitted Rol to sign the document. Rol actually signed his name above Leclerc's, but it was an empty gesture. Both Leclerc and Rol signed on behalf of the French Provisional Government. There was also no mention of the Allies. The entire party then departed from the prefecture to drive to the Gare Montparnasse for the meeting with de Gaulle.

Leclerc and von Choltitz rode together in the same armored vehicle. When they arrived at the Gare Montparnasse, von Choltitz, who was known to have heart problems, suffered a mild attack.

He ran into a small toilet stall and asked for some water so he could take his medication, which he always carried with him. Leclerc's adjunct, Major Weil, who spoke excellent German, gave him a glass of water and said, "General, I hope you don't mean to take poison." Von Choltitz replied, "No, young man. We won't do that." [16]

Leclerc then asked von Choltitz to write an order for his men to stop the fighting. This was especially necessary as most of the strongpoints [*Stützpunkte*] continued to resist. "I composed the order which instructed my soldiers to end the purposeless fight," said von Choltitz.

> Order! The resistance in the sectors of the *Stützpunkte* and within the *Stützpunkte* must cease immediately.
>
> By order of the Commanding General v. Choltitz, General of the Infantry. [17]

Von Choltitz's order was distributed to each strongpoint by a French officer, joined by a member of von Choltitz's staff. It was sufficient to end the resistance at all of the strongpoints except at the Palais du Luxembourg, where the SS continued to hold out. To force the SS to cease their resistance, von Choltitz sent his chief of staff, Colonel Friedrich von Unger, to the Palais. With him went Colonel Jean Crepin, the Second Armored Division's artillery commander. They arrived a little before six-thirty that evening and were shocked by the destruction they saw. Meeting with the SS commander, they told him he had one hour to end his resistance. If his troops did not surrender, "they would not be treated as prisoners of war." The SS commander reluctantly agreed. To his officers he said, "In the name of the Führer" he was ordering a surrender. [18] For the next hour the SS garrison fired off their ammunition. At 7:35 p.m., exactly one hour after Crepin's ultimatum, the gates of the Palais swung open and the German SS troops under a white flag marched out into captivity. With the surrender of this SS garrison, Paris was free of the last German holdouts. Thanks to von Choltitz, it had been achieved without significant damage to the city. When the final results were tallied, 14,800 Germans became prisoners of war. Only 200 had been killed that day. Overall German losses for the five days of resistance approached 3,000, but most of those had been with Aulock outside the city.[19]

Celebrations were everywhere. "A great city in which everyone is happy," wrote famed journalist A. J. Liebling. Ernest Hemingway and his followers, including Colonel David Bruce, went to the Ritz, which was all but deserted. Asked by the manager what they wanted, Hemingway said "seventy-three dry martinis." After which he and Bruce and several others had dinner, which Bruce reported was "superb." Another said, "We drank. We ate. We glowed." And it was the same down the line. A sergeant from Minnesota wrote to his parents, "I have never in my life been kissed so much." The war correspondent Ernie Pyle said, "Paris seems to have all the beautiful girls we have always heard it had. . . . They dress in riotous colors. . . . The liberation is the loveliest, brightest story of our time." And Private Irwin Shaw of the Twelfth Infantry Regiment, who would become a famous novelist after the war, said that August 25 was "the day the war should have ended."[20]

There were problems, but they were not major. The Milice, Vichy's paramilitary organization, was not under von Choltitz and did not surrender. It occupied no buildings, but individual members kept up a brief resistance, firing their weapons from windows and rooftops. Some members of the FFI also posed problems as they also fired independently. Those Parisians who had collaborated with the Germans often found their neighbors upset and seeking revenge, and the women who collaborated horizontally found themselves the victims of self-appointed avengers who beat them, shaved their heads, and paraded them through the streets. But the major resistance was over. Paris had been liberated.

Charles de Gaulle spent the morning of August 25 in Rambouillet. He was in hourly contact with Leclerc, and followed his progress closely. As he said, "I felt myself simultaneously gripped by emotion and filled with serenity." De Gaulle was determined not to allow his power to be infringed. "The mission with which I was invested seemed as clear as it could be."[21]

Shortly after noon, de Gaulle got into an open-top black Hotchkiss convertible for the ride into Paris. Sitting beside him was General Alphonse Juin. They were joined by two more sedans, with a jeep in front and a jeep in back, both jeeps armed with machine guns. Initially the roads were clear, but when the

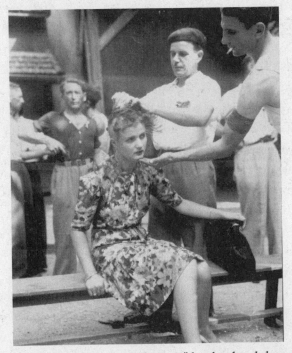

A French "horizontal collaborator" has her head shaved

convoy reached Longjumeau, a market town twenty kilometers south of Paris, the crowds became immense, making passage difficult. When they reached the Porte d'Italie, the wall of spectators became almost impassable. Most had assumed that de Gaulle would go first to the Hôtel de Ville and greet the leadership of the Parisian Committee of National Liberation (CPL) and the National Council of the Resistance headed by Georges Bidault. Instead, he headed for the Gare Montparnasse, where Leclerc was waiting. This was deliberate on de Gaulle's part. He wanted to downplay the importance of the CPL and the National Council of the Resistance and emphasize the role of the French army. It was also his way of deflecting Communist influence.

At the station, de Gaulle greeted Leclerc warmly, delighted that his troops had "brought off a complete victory without the city suffering the demolitions or the population losses that had been feared."[22] In the receiving line were General Chaban-Delmas and Colonel Rol. De Gaulle, who apparently had never met the twenty-nine-year-old Chaban-Delmas before, was surprised at his youth. "Well, I'll be damned," he was heard to mutter.[23] Next was Rol, whom de Gaulle congratulated for having "driven the enemy from our streets, decimated and demoralized his troops, and blockaded his units in their strongholds."[24] De Gaulle was aware of Rol's ability to command the FFI, and wanted to reassure him. He did not want the FFI to become enemies. De Gaulle's son, Philippe, a lieutenant in the Second Armored Division, was also there. De Gaulle kissed his son on both cheeks before he was sent off with a German major to effect the surrender of the German troops at the Palais Bourbon.

After the preliminaries, Leclerc showed de Gaulle the surrender document von Choltitz had signed. When de Gaulle saw Rol's signature, he bristled. "You allowed Rol-Tanguy to sign! Why do you think I made you temporary governor of Paris?"

De Gaulle and Leclerc

"But Chaban agreed," Leclerc replied.

"Even so it is not correct. You are the ranking officer, and consequently solely responsible." De Gaulle did not pursue the matter. It was clear that Leclerc had acted out of goodwill and it was pointless to object. "You have done well," de Gaulle told him. "And I will recommend Rol-Tanguy be made a Companion of Liberation." Turning to a senior reporter for the BBC, de Gaulle said, "The enemy has surrendered to General Leclerc and the French Forces of the Interior."[25] He carefully included the FFI in his statement to defuse the Communist Party, if that was possible. With that, the business at the Gare Montparnasse was finished, and de Gaulle departed for his old office at the Ministry of War.

De Gaulle had decided to make the Ministry of War his headquarters in Paris rather than the Élysée Palace. He had not been elected, and felt that the Élysée Palace was reserved for those who were. He had also served in the Ministry of War before leaving for

London in 1940. When he arrived, he found that his office was exactly as he had left it. The Germans had not occupied the Ministry of War, so the furniture and everything else was unchanged. "Gigantic events had overturned the world. Our Army was annihilated. France had virtually collapsed. But at the Ministry of War, the look of things remained immutable. . . . The vestibule, the staircase, the arms hanging on the walls—were just as they had been. Here, in person, were the same stewards and ushers. I entered the 'minister's office,' which M. Paul Reynaud and I had left together on the night of June 10, 1940. Not a piece of furniture, not a rug, not a curtain had been disturbed. . . . Nothing was missing except the State. It was my duty to restore it: I installed my staff at once and got down to work."[26]

De Gaulle was moving with confidence. He immediately ordered the French officials in Algiers and London to get to Paris as soon as possible, and also arranged for the transfer of eight thousand small arms from the Americans to the Paris police to replace the weapons they had lost.

Shortly after his arrival at the Ministry he was called on by Charles Luizet and Alexandre Parodi, who urged him to go and speak to the National Council of the Resistance and the Parisian Committee of Liberation at the Hôtel de Ville. They were waiting for him, said Parodi. De Gaulle, who was still determined to deemphasize the two groups, refused. They were simply the symbols of municipal authority. He was the government of France. De Gaulle was intensely afraid of fueling a Communist takeover, and believed that ignoring the CNR and the CPL was the best way to avoid one. Parodi and Luizet continued to press the case. Finally, de Gaulle yielded. "All right, if we must go, let's go!"[27] But before leaving he made two decisions. He would visit the *préfecture de police* before going to Hôtel de Ville, and tomorrow he would lead a gigantic parade down the Champs-Élysées to Notre-Dame and symbolize his official entry into Paris. De Gaulle believed it was essential to demonstrate the support he had and leave the Communist Party in the lurch.

De Gaulle arrived at the *préfecture* at 7 p.m. He was greeted by a packed courtyard of police, "trembling with joy and pride," and the police band, which kept up a steady stream of marches. De Gaulle had deliberately chosen to visit the *préfecture* first to demonstrate his support for the police and to thank them for leading the insurrection, thereby "increasing their prestige and their popularity," and making up for their "long humiliation."[28] Also, by calling on the police, he was solidifying his base should problems ensue. It was de Gaulle at his best.

From the *préfecture*, de Gaulle went on foot to the Hôtel de Ville. He was accompanied by Parodi, Juin, Luizet, and André Le Troquer, his commissioner for war. Again they were greeted by a vast outpouring of Parisians. At the Hôtel de Ville, the demonstration was even greater. "On the steps, the combatants, tears in their eyes, presented arms. Beneath a unified chorus of cheers, I was led to the center of the salon on the first floor. Here were grouped the members of the National Council of the Resistance and the Parisian Committee of Liberation. . . . All wore the Cross of Lorraine. Glancing around the group vibrant with enthusiasm, affection, and curiosity, I felt we had immediately recognized one another, that there was among us, combatants of the same battle, an incomparable link, and that if there were divergences of policy and ambition among us, the fact that the majority and I found ourselves together would carry the rest of us along with us. . . . I did not see a single gesture or hear a single word which was not one of perfect dignity. How admirable the success of a meeting long dreamed of and paid for with so many efforts, disappointments, and deaths."[29]

Georges Maranne, a Communist, spoke first, on behalf of the

Parisian Committee of Liberation. He welcomed de Gaulle to Paris in glowing terms. He was followed by Georges Bidault, head of the National Council of the Resistance, who was even more eloquent in his welcome. De Gaulle was then asked to speak—not just to those inside the Hôtel de Ville, but to the vast crowd that had gathered outside as well. Without any preparations, de Gaulle stepped outside into the crowd and gave what many believe was the most effective speech of his lifetime.

> Paris! Paris outraged! Paris broken! Paris martyred! But Paris liberated! Liberated by itself, liberated by its people with the help of the French armies, with the support and the help of all France, of the France that fights, of the only France, of the real France, of the eternal France!
>
> Since the enemy which held Paris has capitulated into our hands, France returns to Paris, to her home. She returns bloody, but quite resolute. She returns there enlightened by the immense lesson, but more certain than ever of her duties and of her rights.
>
> I speak of her duties first, and I will sum them all up by saying that for now it is a matter of the duties of war. The enemy is staggering, but he is not beaten yet. He remains on our soil.
>
> It will not even be enough that we have, with the help of our dear and admirable Allies, chased him from our home for us to consider ourselves satisfied after what has happened. We want to enter his territory as is fitting, as victors.
>
> This is why the French vanguard has entered Paris with guns blazing. This is why the great French army from Italy has landed in the south and is advancing rapidly up the Rhône valley. This is why our brave and dear forces of the interior are going to arm themselves with modern weapons.

It is for this revenge, this vengeance and justice, that we will keep fighting until the last day, until the day of total and complete victory.

This duty of war, all the men who are here and all those who hear us in France know that it demands national unity. We, who have lived the greatest hours of our history, we have nothing else to wish than to show ourselves, up to the end, worthy of France. *Vive la France!*[30]

It was a magnificent address. De Gaulle had spoken extemporaneously and had captured the hour. Bidault was so moved that on the verge of tears he asked de Gaulle to proclaim the Republic. "General, here around you are the National Council of Resistance and the Parisian Committee of Liberation. We ask you formally to proclaim the Republic before the people who have gathered here."[31]

De Gaulle speaking at the Hôtel de Ville

It was a moving request, but de Gaulle was not interested. "The Republic has never ceased to exist," he replied. "Free France, Fighting France, the French Committee of National Liberation have successfully incorporated it. Vichy always was and still remains null and void. I myself am the President of the government of the Republic. Why should I proclaim it now?"[32] De Gaulle was not only correct, but by standing firm reinforced his position as head of the French State. He wished to emphasize that Pétain's regime was an aberration, and that *he* represented French legitimacy. He also wanted to downplay the possibility of another Paris Commune. As a leading biographer has written, "De Gaulle was a blend of strength, diversity, and ruthlessness. At the Hôtel de Ville, he had just uttered one of the most fervent cries of love that a town has ever inspired; now he regained his control and resumed the direction of the matter point by point."[33]

After his appearance at the Hôtel de Ville, de Gaulle returned to the Ministry of War, where he began to plan the parade he had scheduled for the next day. At the same time, General Pierre Koenig, whom de Gaulle had just appointed to be military governor of Paris, hosted a dinner for the senior officers of the Second Armored Division, at the grand mess room of Les Invalides—the building containing the tomb of Napoléon. Walking over to Les Invalides that evening, Leclerc turned to Colonel Boissieu and said, "You know, Boissieu, it is extraordinary to have liberated Paris without destroying any of its riches! All the bridges, all the buildings, all the artistic treasures are still intact. What luck we've had. Do you remember that day you brought me that letter from General de Gaulle with my mission to liberate Paris? . . . Well, that document, I still have on me, in this pocket. It is there with another letter from General de Gaulle. Whenever I felt unhappy or doubtful, I reread them."[34]

More to the point, during the meal the discussion focused on the role of the Resistance in Paris's liberation, lingering over the details of the cease-fire and the role of the Communist Party. It was a useful exchange. When the meal ended, General Koenig said, "We have narrowly avoided another Paris Commune."[35] It was clear on the evening of August 25 that not only had the Germans been defeated, but so too had the Communists. And de Gaulle deserved the credit.

For most Parisians, the issue that evening was not Communism but enjoying their new freedom. The Germans were gone, and Paris was open as it had not been for four years. The celebrations went on long into the night. As a Frenchwoman put it, "Many Parisian women were too charitable to let our lads spend their first night in the capital alone."[36] And it was not just French soldiers who were embraced. As Ernie Pyle put it, "Anybody who does not sleep with a woman tonight is just an exhibitionist."[37] At the close of the day, Albert Camus may have said it best when he wrote, "Those who never despaired of themselves or their country can find tonight under this sky their recompense."[38]

— X —

De Gaulle Triumphant

"What I wanted to see was the situation in Paris under control, and as far as I was concerned de Gaulle was the best man to do that."

—DWIGHT D. EISENHOWER, AUGUST 27, 1944

S aturday, August 26, dawned bright and clear. It was another perfect day. And de Gaulle was satisfied and proud. Not only had Paris been liberated, but it had been done with few casualties and little damage. Even more important, it had been done with a united France. There was no threat of another Paris Commune, or any other challenge to de Gaulle's authority. The parade down the Champs-Élysées that he was planning would be a fitting demonstration of this achievement. News of the pending parade was spread throughout Paris by the radio, the press, and word of mouth. The enthusiasm of the Parisians was unanimous. Even *L'Humanité* was outspoken in its support. With massive headlines on the front page, the Communist paper said: "AT 15:00, FROM THE ARC DE TRIOMPHE TO NOTRE DAME, THE PEOPLE WILL UNANIMOUSLY ACCLAIM GENERAL DE GAULLE."[1]

The only opposition came from the American military. The American commanders wanted to pursue the retreating Germans, not parade through Paris. On the evening of the 25th, Major General Leonard Gerow, commanding V Corps, ordered Leclerc to make contact with the German forces northeast of Paris and prepare to attack them. Leclerc took the order to de Gaulle, who was not only surprised but upset. He told Leclerc to designate a small unit that could guard against any German approach, but hold the rest of his division for the parade: "Since the Allied command had not resolved to make the slightest liaison with me, I ordered Leclerc to inform it of the arrangements I had decided on. . . . To the contrary orders that the Allies might send, Leclerc was to reply that he was maintaining his position according to General de Gaulle's orders."[2]

When Gerow heard Leclerc's response, he became livid. The following morning, he sent a letter to Leclerc ordering him to ignore de Gaulle's instructions and head northeast immediately.

> You are operating under my direct command and will not accept orders from any other source. I understand you have been directed by General de Gaulle to parade your troops this afternoon at 1400 hours. You will disregard those orders and continue on the present mission assigned you of clearing up all resistance in Paris and environs within your zone of action.
>
> Your command will not participate in the parade this afternoon or at any other time except on orders signed by me personally.[3]

The American colonel who gave Gerow's letter to Leclerc said that if the Second Armored Division participated in the parade that afternoon, Gerow would consider it a "formal breach of military discipline." Leclerc took the colonel to de Gaulle, who dismissed Gerow's order. "I loaned you Leclerc," said de Gaulle. "Surely I can borrow him back for a few moments."[4] In his memoirs, de Gaulle said, "Naturally I ignored this order." He went on to point out that except for Gerow, the Allies did not "meddle with affairs in the capital."[5] Gerow did not understand the political significance of the parade, and not surprisingly he was ignored.

The crowds in Paris gathered all day to watch the parade. De Gaulle estimated that almost two million people—an unprecedented number—turned out between the Arc de Triomphe and the Place de la Concorde. At 3 p.m. de Gaulle arrived at the Arc de Triomphe, where he was saluted by the *Régiment de Marche du Tchad*, the oldest unit of the Free French Army, originally commanded by Leclerc in Chad. He moved immediately to the Tomb of the Unknown Soldier under the Arc, placed a wreath of gladiolas in the shape of the Cross of Lorraine on the grave, and relit

General de Gaulle laying a wreath at the Tomb of the Unknown Soldier

the eternal flame that had been extinguished when the Germans occupied Paris in June 1940.

The parade was ready to begin. Preceded by four Sherman tanks of Leclerc's division, de Gaulle led the way. He was joined by his generals—Juin, Koenig, and Leclerc—as well as the leaders of the Paris Resistance, Colonel Rol and Maurice Kriegel-Valrimont; the members of the government Alexandre Parodi, Charles Luizet, Chaban-Delmas; and Georges Bidault of the CNR and Charles Tillon of the Parisian Committee of Liberation. It was a complete collection of the leaders of the Paris liberation, with de Gaulle leading the way. With his six-foot-five stature, he easily dominated the scene. They did not ride in vehicles but walked in the center of the Champs-Élysées from the Arc de Triomphe to the Place de la Concorde. They were followed by the troops of the Second Armored Division, and then by members of the Resistance.

The immense crowd roared approval. Young girls frequently ran out to give de Gaulle bouquets of flowers, which he graciously accepted. At the statue to Georges Clemenceau, midway down the Champs-Élysées, de Gaulle paused and saluted. "What a triumph," said Bidault. "Yes, but what a crowd," de Gaulle replied. As Simone de Beauvoir noted, "We acclaimed not a military parade, but a popular carnival, disorganized and magnificent."[6]

De Gaulle was visibly moved. "I went on, touched and yet tranquil, amid the inexpressible exultation of the crowd, beneath the storm of voices echoing my name, trying, as I advanced, to look at every person in all that multitude in order that every eye might register my presence, raising and lowering my arms to reply to the acclamation: this was one of those miracles of national consciousness, one of those gestures which sometimes, in the course of centuries, illuminate the history of France."[7]

When de Gaulle reached the Place de la Concorde, the mood

*General de Gaulle leading the parade. General Koenig is
on his left; General Leclerc follows.*

was briefly broken when shots rang out. De Gaulle continued to
march across the square as though nothing had happened, to a
convertible automobile that was to take him to Notre-Dame. Most
spectators in the square, however, dove for cover. They watched in
amazement as de Gaulle carried on while the gunfire continued.
To this day it is not known who was doing the shooting—or what
they were shooting at. As a Paris reporter said, de Gaulle's behavior "inspired confidence and compassion at the same time. His
face was the face of a hero."[8]

At Notre-Dame the situation was tense. Monsignor Emmanuel Suhard, the cardinal-archbishop of Paris, had been instructed
to stay away from the proceedings because of his support for the

Vichy regime.* He had welcomed Pétain to Paris in April, and in July had presided over the funeral of Phillipe Henriot, the Vichy minister of information and an ardent pro-Nazi who had been assassinated by the Resistance. De Gaulle said he understood Suhard's actions because the Church always accepted the "established order" and he was "not unaware of the fact that the cardinal's piety and charity were so immense that they left little room in his soul for the appreciation of temporal matters."[9] But he accepted Parodi's request that Suhard remain in his residence during the ceremony because he did not want any protests during it, and above all wanted to keep the Communists in line.

De Gaulle got out of his car at the Hôtel de Ville, was received by *Garde républicaine* in dress uniform while the band played *La Marseillaise*, and then walked across the Pont d'Arcole to the cathedral. Again the crowd was immense, and again, once de Gaulle crossed the bridge, shots rang out, apparently coming from the towers of Notre-Dame. As happened at the Place de la Concorde, the crowd ran for cover, but de Gaulle, accompanied by his generals and government officials, continued without flinching. "It was the most extraordinary example of courage I have ever seen," said Robert Reid, a BBC reporter who was covering the event.[10] Troops from Leclerc's division returned the gunfire, and order was quickly restored.

---

* Emmanuel Célestin Suhard was named cardinal by Pope Pius XI in 1935. In May 1940, Pius XII appointed him archbishop of Paris. In that capacity Suhard vigorously supported the formation of the Vichy regime under Pétain, and remained a powerful advocate, except that in July 1942 he wrote a public protest against the deportation of the Jews from Paris. He was briefly confined to the archbishop's residence by the Nazis, but that was soon lifted. After the war he became the president of the Assembly of Cardinals and Archbishops of France, and the official spokesman of the Church of France. He was also instrumental in establishing the Worker-Priest movement after the war, which was an attempt to bring the clergy closer to the people. He died on May 30, 1949, at the age of seventy-five.

Inside the cathedral the congregation was waiting, but as soon as de Gaulle entered, firing began again. Rather than being directed at anyone, however, it simply went into the air, over the congregants' heads. Once again people sought cover. And again de Gaulle continued to walk deliberately, to his place of honor at the left of the transept. Because of the electricity outage there were no lights and no organ music, but the service went on. De Gaulle was greeted by Suhard's replacement, Monsignor Brot, who told de Gaulle that the cardinal was upset he was not welcome at the ceremony. De Gaulle said he would meet with Suhard soon. Although some firing continued, General Koenig, standing behind de Gaulle, shouted at the congregation, "Have you no pride? Stand up."[11] As people rose to their feet, the clergy began to

De Gaulle and Monsignor Brot at Notre-Dame

sing the *Magnificat*. De Gaulle led the response. It was even more impressive. As Helen Kirkpatrick, a reporter for the *Chicago Daily News*, wrote to her family, "I am not one for believing in miracles, but only a miracle prevented those French generals, and myself as well I suppose, from being killed."[12]

When the *Magnificat* was completed, and with shots still ringing out, de Gaulle decided to terminate the ceremony. He walked out of the cathedral with his head up and shoulders back, the symbol of France reborn. Whatever had caused the shooting—and its source remains unknown—de Gaulle emerged as the unquestioned leader of the new France. His poise and bravery were now a matter of record, and were unparalleled in modern French history. As an American newsman wrote, "de Gaulle had France in the palm of his hand."[13]

On his way back to the War Ministry after Notre-Dame, de Gaulle decided to take advantage of the shootings and disarm the Resistance in Paris. He did not believe that the shootings were done by members of the Vichy Militia or German stay-behinds, but rather by the FFI, to emphasize the danger that Paris faced. "By shooting a few bullets into the air at the agreed upon hour, without perhaps foreseeing the bursts of fire that would be the consequence, an attempt had been made to create the impression that certain threats were still lurking in the shadows [and] that the resistance organizations must remain armed and vigilant."[14] When he arrived at the War Ministry, he instructed General Koenig to see to it that the FFI in Paris was disarmed and that the members who wished to join the regular army were enrolled as soon as possible.

Koenig immediately went to see Colonel Richard Vissering of SHAEF. "The worst danger in Paris at the moment is the FFI," said Koenig. The best way to relieve the situation was to get "the most disturbing elements into uniform and under military discipline."

Koenig asked Vissering for fifteen thousand uniforms so that the FFI could be taken into the army. Vissering agreed. Reporting the request to SHAEF headquarters, he said, "The situation from a public safety standpoint is alarming. Citizens of all kinds go about in fear of being arrested by one gang or another. It appears most of these groups are political, the most powerful among those being Communist. The region is rapidly becoming a terrorist one and the general opinion on all sides is that a civil war may break out at any moment."[15] De Gaulle was taking advantage of the shooting to further consolidate his position.

The sense of victory was disturbed Saturday evening when the Germans attacked Paris from the air. At 11:15 p.m., German bombers from Luftwaffe bases in eastern France and Holland appeared over the city and began to drop their bombs. There were few anti-aircraft guns available, and the Germans had control of the skies. The bombs were dropped largely in northern Paris. In the end 214 persons were killed and 597 buildings damaged, including the Halle aux Vins and the Moulin de Paris—the city's most famous wine center and flour mill. Hitler had again ordered the destruction of the city, and this time General Otto Dessloch complied. It was the largest air raid of the war on Paris and served as a reminder that hostilities were not over.

From his desk in the War Ministry that evening, de Gaulle wrote to Eisenhower to thank him for assigning the capture of Paris to the Leclerc division. "Although Paris is in the best order possible after all that has happened, it is absolutely necessary to leave a French division here for the time being. Until other big units arrive from the south, I ask you to keep the Leclerc division here." De Gaulle went on to point out that the food situation in Paris was serious and that there was a severe lack of coal. "Thanks in advance for whatever you can do to remedy this."[16]

Eisenhower had thus far stayed out of the picture. He wanted de Gaulle to reap the benefits, and the best way to do that was to remain absent. But he was deeply concerned about what was happening. Because he was the Allied supreme commander, the situation was ultimately his responsibility. And based on his experience in North Africa, he understood that it was best not to interfere and to allow de Gaulle to handle it.

Early Saturday morning, after the liberation was complete, Eisenhower decided he would go into the city and pay tribute to de Gaulle. Doing so publicly would further enhance de Gaulle's position. Still at his headquarters in Tournièrs, he and his driver Kay Summersby left late that morning for Bradley's headquarters in Chartres, a six-hour trip. They went through the Falaise battlefield for a second time, and Kay said, "I was glad when we emerged from the Falaise section, leaving the sickly odor and sight of death far behind."[17] They passed through Gacé, the tactical headquarters of Montgomery's Twenty-First Army Group, and Ike stopped to invite Montgomery to join him. Montgomery was not there but later sent a short message to Eisenhower declining. He was too busy, he said. Why Montgomery refused has often been speculated upon, and some writers assume he was obeying British Foreign Office instructions to stay away so that Ike's call on de Gaulle "would be an undiluted American gesture of recognition."[18] Eisenhower was not disappointed that Montgomery declined. "It's just as well," he told Summersby. "The less I see of him, the better it is for my blood pressure."[19]

When Eisenhower and Kay arrived at his headquarters in Chartres that afternoon, Bradley wasn't there. He was in Brest, on a quick inspection visit, but he returned soon after they arrived. According to Bradley, "Ike suggested we slip quietly into Paris for a glimpse of the city the following morning. 'It's Sunday,' he said. 'Europe will be sleeping late. We can do it without any fuss.'"[20] Bradley agreed. That evening Ike, Bradley, Kay, and Colonel

James Gault, Eisenhower's British aide, enjoyed dinner together. "We had a marvelous evening," Summersby wrote. "Bradley and Ike got along very well, almost like brothers." Dinner was simply rations and wine. "We played a little bridge, talked a bit. That was all."[21] Bradley's aide, Lieutenant Colonel Chester Hansen, said that though Eisenhower would never admit it, "I know he was anxious to see the city. Kay certainly was; she seemed the most concerned about it. . . . Brad was not too keen on going. Told me he would never go if Ike hadn't come up and asked him."[22]

It was obvious that Eisenhower was not only interested in buttressing de Gaulle's authority, but also wanted to see Paris. His tour with Pershing on the Battle Monuments Commission had ended in August 1929—exactly fifteen years earlier—and he was eager to see how the city had changed. "We lived on the Right Bank near the river," he told Kay. "I often used to walk up to the Arc de Triomphe with John [Ike's son], but nobody gave me a second look in those days."[23]

The drive into Paris on Sunday morning was lengthy. Kay drove Eisenhower's official Cadillac adorned with American, British, and French flags, and as people recognized Ike, the crowds became enormous. Colonel Hansen reported that when the convoy reached the city, people who had been asleep "came out in their pajamas to wave *bonjour* at us. Flags and shouting everywhere and the enthusiasm was infectious."[24] They were met at the Porte d'Orléans by General Gerow and General Koenig and escorted to de Gaulle's headquarters in the Ministry of War.

Kay Summersby describes the scene they encountered. "On the surface, the city looked just as it had when I left there in August of 1939. The tree-lined sidewalks, the unbombed houses, the broad thoroughfares . . . all these were the same. But many a street was blocked by crude barricades, where the people of Paris had started their own liberation. Along some areas were burned, overturned German vehicles. The only cars were those operated by mad-eyed FFI men who careened through the streets . . . firing their guns whenever the spirit (or a new bottle) moved them. Tanks and other armored vehicles of General Jacques Leclerc's force roamed the avenues with a festive air immediately contagious. . . . The sidewalks were packed with crowds who shouted and threw kisses at our convoy." [25]

It was Eisenhower's decision to call on de Gaulle, and it was very well thought out—the supreme commander of Allied Forces paying tribute to the president of France. "I did this very deliberately as a kind of de facto recognition of de Gaulle as the provisional President of France," said Ike. "He was very grateful—he never forgot that. After all, I was commanding every damn thing on the continent. He looked on it as . . . a very definite recognition of his high political position and place. That, of course, was what he wanted and what Roosevelt had never given him." [26]

Once again Eisenhower and de Gaulle hit it off. De Gaulle presented Eisenhower with a list of urgent needs—food, gasoline, military uniforms for the members of the Resistance who would be taken into the French army. He also asked for additional military equipment for new divisions he planned to create.

In addition to the logistical help, de Gaulle asked Ike for the temporary loan of two American divisions as a show of force and to bolster his position. "I understood his problem," said Eisenhower, "and while I had no spare units to station temporarily in Paris, I did promise him that two of our divisions, marching to the front, would do so through the main avenues of the city. I suggested that while these divisions were passing through Paris they could proceed in ceremonial formation and invited him to review them. . . . I told him that General Bradley would come back to the city and stand with him on the reviewing platform to symbolize Allied unity."

Under Eisenhower's orders, two days later the Twenty-Eighth Infantry Division and the Fifth Armored Division marched down the Champs-Élysées on their way to the front lines east of Paris. The photo of the Twenty-Eighth Infantry marching was immediately placed on an American postage stamp. As Eisenhower said later, "Because this ceremonial march coincided exactly with the local battle plan it became possibly the only instance in history of troops marching in parade through the capital of a great country to participate in pitched battle the same day."[27]

De Gaulle told Eisenhower he was very dissatisfied with General Gerow, and that he planned to keep Leclerc's division in Paris for several more days. Eisenhower, an old friend of Gerow, did not object. He realized Gerow was not familiar with the political scene. And so Leclerc's division stayed in Paris until the beginning of September. While he was in Paris, Leclerc wrote to General Haislip asking that his division be taken from V Corps and reassigned to XV Corps. Haislip and Patton were strongly in favor, and on September 6, when the Second Armored Division went

Twenty-Eighth Infantry marching down the Champs-Élysées

back into combat, it was with XV Corps. On September 12 the division attacked German Panzers near Dompaire and scored a major victory. Haislip called it a "brilliant example" of air-ground coordination. Patton personally presented Leclerc with a Silver Star. But Leclerc's most significant achievement was the capture of Strasbourg in November, which solidified French control of Alsace. The Second Armored was also the first Allied unit to reach Hitler's lair at Berchtesgaden. For his service commanding the Second Armored Division, Leclerc was awarded the Grand Cross of the Legion of Honor.*

Eisenhower told de Gaulle that he planned to move his headquarters to Versailles. This was very much to de Gaulle's liking. "I approved the move," de Gaulle wrote in his memoirs, "believing it was advantageous to have the Allied commander in chief not lodged in Paris but useful that he be nearby."[28] Eisenhower's decision to place Allied headquarters in Versailles was another example of his deference to de Gaulle. He knew that if he was in Paris, he would steal the limelight from de Gaulle, and that was something he wanted to avoid.

Eisenhower and de Gaulle parted on the best terms possible. "I expressed to this great and good leader the esteem, confidence, and gratitude of the French government," said de Gaulle.[29] Eisenhower was equally supportive. "What I wanted to see was the situation in Paris under control, and as far as I was concerned de Gaulle was the best man to do that. I wanted my visit to show the people he had my support, that as far as I was concerned de Gaulle was the boss of France. That's the effect I wanted and that's the effect I got."[30]

---

* After the war Leclerc served in Indochina and then in Algeria. Appointed inspector of land forces in Africa, he was killed in a plane crash in Algeria in November 1947. His funeral service was held at Notre-Dame and he was buried at Les Invalides. On August 23, 1952—the anniversary of his drive on Paris—he was posthumously made a marshal of France.

From the War Ministry, Eisenhower and Bradley initially went to Les Invalides, and Ike met first with Gerow, then with Koenig. Eisenhower understood de Gaulle's concern about Gerow, and fortunately he and Gerow were old friends from the prewar army. In their meeting, Eisenhower brought Gerow up to date on the political situation and told him Paris was not to be governed by the American military but by the French. Ike told him to hand over his office to Koenig and get back to the front fighting Germans as soon as possible. He also said that Leclerc's division was going back to Patton and Haislip. Gerow was not offended and rather pleased to be going back into action. There were no hard feelings. To Koenig, Ike said essentially the same. The next day Gerow visited Koenig and told him he was turning Paris over to him. Koenig was caustic. "The French authorities alone have handled the administration of the city of Paris since its liberation. Acting as the military governor of Paris since my arrival, I assumed the responsibilities . . . the 25th of August, 1944." [31]

Gerow went back to the front,* and Eisenhower later joked about it to Marshall: "We have had some little trouble with de Gaulle and Leclerc in Paris but Gerow handled it firmly and I rushed in there Sunday morning for an hour to back him up. I guess we should not blame the French for getting a bit hysterical under the conditions, and I must say they seem now to be settling down in good order." [32] Eisenhower was superb at writing communiques to justify his action, and this is one example. He

---

* Leonard Gerow was one of the outstanding combat commanders of World War II. He remained in command of V Corps until January 15, 1945, when he was given command of the newly established Fifteenth Army. He was promoted to lieutenant general on February 6, 1945. After the war he commanded the army's Command and General Staff School, and on January 1, 1948, became commanding general of Second Army. He retired in July 1950, and four years later was appointed a full general on Eisenhower's recommendation by Act of Congress (Public Law 83-508).

Eisenhower with Bradley and Koenig at the Arc de Triomphe

had backed de Gaulle, not Gerow, but everything was handled successfully.

From the Invalides, Eisenhower and Bradley were taken by Koenig across the Seine to the Place de la Concorde and up the Champs-Élysées to the Arc de Triomphe. The crowds were enormous. A great roar went up when Eisenhower was recognized. "Eisenhower! Eisenhower!" they chanted as French and American MPs tried to clear a path to the Tomb of the Unknown Soldier. After paying their respects, Eisenhower and Bradley attempted to return to their car. It was almost impossible to move through the crowd. Eisenhower was kissed on both cheeks by a large Frenchman as he approached his car, and Bradley—who had broken off and was headed for a jeep—by a beautiful young woman. "Later, as I rubbed a smear of her lipstick from my cheek, I joked with Ike about my better fortune. 'I'll leave the accolades to you and take my chances with the crowd.'"[33]

Eisenhower and Bradley then headed back to Bradley's headquarters for a late lunch. The visit to Paris was a moving experience. Kay Summersby may have expressed it best. "I hate lofty, dramatic words. But there in Paris that August day—a Paris still resounding to liberating gunfire, a Paris absolutely wild with mass happiness over something intangible called Freedom—I knew exactly what the war was all about."[34]

But the FFI in Paris remained a problem. On Monday, August 28, de Gaulle summoned the leaders of the Resistance to the War Department. As he wrote later, "The iron was hot: I struck."[35] De Gaulle congratulated the leaders for their role in liberating Paris, and then said that since the fighting was over, he was dissolving the FFI. Members who wished to join the French army could do so immediately. He also said that since the liberation struggle was over, the National Council of the Resistance no longer had a raison d'être. The Parisian Committee of Liberation was also to disappear. Georges Bidault, the head of the CNR, would immediately become France's foreign minister, and Charles Tillon, who headed the CPL and who was Communist, would become the government's minister of air. De Gaulle handled it well.

Perhaps the most useful result was that Colonel Rol, who did not disagree with de Gaulle, immediately organized a battalion of FFI members and joined the French army as part of the 151st Infantry Regiment. The battalion did well in combat, and in June 1945, after the war ended, Rol received the Croix de la Libération from de Gaulle himself. Later Rol was made the commander of the occupation force in the city of Coblenz in the French Zone of Occupation in Germany. At the end of his duties in Coblenz, Rol was inducted into the French Legion of Honor.

De Gaulle was in control. More than eleven thousand members of the FFI joined the army, and on September 9 de Gaulle established a new provisional government with twenty-one ministers, including Bidault and Tillon. In many respects, this was the informal beginning of the Fourth Republic, which did not officially come into existence until October 13, 1946. De Gaulle's role in avoiding civil strife in Paris is important. Not only did he keep the Communists in the government, but also in October he pardoned Maurice Thorez, the head of the French Communist Party, who had spent the war years in Moscow. Drafted into the French army in 1939, Thorez had deserted and fled to the Soviet Union. The army responded by trying him for desertion and sentencing him to death. De Gaulle, who had been similarly sentenced under Vichy, saw no problem in pardoning Thorez, who returned to France in November 1944 as head of the Communist Party and became a staunch supporter of de Gaulle.

It should also be noted that Moscow did not seek to overthrow the French government. Stalin did not want a civil war to break out in the West that might divert the Americans and British in the war against Germany. De Gaulle also got along well with Soviet Foreign Minister Molotov. French historians tend to see the avoidance of another Commune entirely in French terms. But the French Communist Party was a loyal subordinate of Moscow, and if the Russians did not want another Commune, the French Party was not going to launch one.

The liberation of Paris was an extraordinary event, but it did not solve many of the problems from which the city suffered in August 1944. Food remained the most serious concern. The American army did its best to provide assistance and, in the fall and winter following liberation, provided more than half of all supplies brought into the city. But as late as January 1945, most Parisians were living on just twelve hundred calories a day. Coal, gas, and heating oil were also in short supply, making Paris very cold in the winter of 1944–45. In the immediate aftermath of liberation, those who had collaborated with the Germans also found life difficult. They were ruthlessly attacked by gangs in Paris who roamed streets looking for collaborators. More than 10,000 were arrested and sent to prisons where Jewish prisoners had been held. As has been mentioned, French women were also punished for their romantic alliances with Germans—more than 100,000 *enfants de Boche* had been born—although for most it was a relatively harmless affair. These were problems the Gaullist government faced, but the larger problem of political stability had been resolved.

When all is said and done, the liberation of a largely undamaged Paris was primarily the work of three men: von Choltitz, de Gaulle, and Eisenhower. Von Choltitz rejected direct orders from Hitler to destroy the city, and he did so knowing that his wife and children might be made to pay for his disobedience. De Gaulle did so as the president of liberated France. He was absolute in his quest for authority, and Paris was essential to his effort. For Eisenhower, who made the ultimate decision to liberate the city, it marked the end of his command apprenticeship and the beginning of his power as a world statesman. On his own authority, without seeking the approval of the Combined Chiefs of Staff, the British government, or Washington, he saved Paris for the French and avoided its destruction. He outmaneuvered FDR and the State Department so skillfully that he left no fingerprints.

All three men were superb military professionals. They understood their duty and fulfilled their responsibility to the utmost. For de Gaulle and Eisenhower, it was just the beginning. De

Gaulle remained as the head of France until January 1946, when he stepped down. He returned in 1958 as the last premier of the Fourth Republic, settled the problems in Algeria, and founded the Fifth Republic with a strong chief executive (he actually wrote the Constitution). De Gaulle served as president from the inception of the Fifth Republic in January 1959 until April 1969. And the Fifth Republic of France has been remarkably stable and successful.

Eisenhower served as president of the United States for two terms. He ended the war in Korea, refused to use nuclear weapons at Dien Bien Phu or to protect the Chinese Nationalist islands, built the Interstate Highway System, and advanced the end of segregation in the South when he sent the 101st Airborne Division to Little Rock in 1957. And the friendship between de Gaulle

De Gaulle at Eisenhower's casket

and Eisenhower continued. When Ike passed away on March 28, 1969, de Gaulle, who was still president of the Fifth Republic, flew to Washington to pay final respects to his wartime ally who lay in state in the Rotunda of the Capitol.

Von Choltitz's career ended in August 1944 when he surrendered Paris. He was never tried for war crimes and after his release from captivity in 1947, he became a hero to the French. He and General Pierre Koenig, who was the military governor of the French zone in Germany and living in Baden-Baden, became good friends. When von Choltitz died in 1966, the French not only provided the guard of honor at his funeral, but the ranking generals in the French army also attended.

A final question is whether the liberation of Paris prolonged the war. The needs of the city, ranging from food to coal, gas, and oil were enormous, and kept the Allied supply forces busy. And in that respect, it did contribute to lengthening the war. But it was not the major factor. As supreme commander, Eisenhower saw the war in political terms. He wanted to avoid a rebirth of Nazism, and believed a total victory was essential for that purpose. The defeat of the German army was not as important as bringing home the defeat to everyone in Germany. Accordingly, after the liberation of Paris, Ike favored a broad frontal advance.

In early September 1944 he rejected the idea that Allied forces would come together north of the Ardennes in a reverse Schlieffen Plan and storm into Germany—as Montgomery cabled it, "a solid mass of forty divisions that would be so strong that it need fear nothing."[36] He also rejected Bradley's proposal for a single thrust led by the American Twelfth Army Group south of the Ardennes into the Saar and the Frankfurt Gap. Rather than choose between the two, Eisenhower adopted both. And he also sent the Sixth Army Group, which had come up from Marseilles under General Jacob Devers against the Germans on the front between

*Colonel d'Omezon, the French commander in
Baden-Baden, salutes von Choltitz's casket*

Bradley and the Swiss border. This was the broad front strategy he believed in. But by not concentrating his forces, he gave the Germans time to regroup.

As a result of Eisenhower's decision, the Allies inched forward along a 450-mile front from Basel to Antwerp. And the Germans, who had effectively been defeated in August, were able to bounce back. Field Marshal von Rundstedt was recalled by Hitler, and in December the Germans launched a counterattack in the Ardennes (*Herbstnebel*), which the Americans called "the Battle of the Bulge." It was eventually contained, but the war went on until May 1945.

Were those extra six months avoidable? It is a question often asked. In many respects a similar situation existed during the

American Civil War. In 1878, on a world tour after his presidency, Ulysses Grant called on Chancellor Otto von Bismarck in Berlin. Bismarck commiserated about the Civil War and told Grant it was terrible. "It had to be terrible," Grant replied. "There had to be an end to slavery. We were fighting an enemy with whom we could not make peace. We had to destroy him. No treaty was possible—only destruction."

"It was a long war," Bismarck replied. "I suppose that means a long peace."[37]

The same applies to Germany. Her total defeat has meant there has been no "stab in the back" myth such as the one that poisoned German history after World War I. There has been little nostalgia for Hitler or the Nazi regime. Eisenhower insisted on a total victory. That may have extended the war by six months, but as Bismarck told Grant, that has meant "a long peace."

Acknowledgments

My principal indebtedness is to Kristen Pack of the Veterans Administration hospital in Huntington. I write in longhand on yellow legal pads. I am eighty-six and my handwriting is not what it once was. Kristen reads what I have written and types it flawlessly. She gives me clean copy every day. She typed many drafts faultlessly and without complaint, and I am deeply indebted. Kristen also prepared the bibliography, did a wonderful job helping to find the pictures we have used, and was a pleasure to work with. I have been privileged to have her work on the book.

I am also deeply indebted to President Jerome Gilbert of Marshall University. I retired from the University of Toronto in 1998, and from Marshall in 2012. My last book was written at Columbia and Georgetown. After that I returned to Huntington, West Virginia, and President Gilbert asked me to become the John Marshall Professor of Political Science emeritus at Marshall, which I did. President Gilbert gave me an office and full university support, for which I am very grateful. I am also indebted to Professor James Leonard of the Geography Department, who drew the four maps in the text.

Once again my editor at Simon & Schuster was Bob Bender. Bob was my editor for *Grant* and *Bush*, and he does a wonderful job. His comments are invaluable and his thoughtfulness is breathtaking. I am also indebted to his assistant, Johanna Li, who is an associate editor at Simon & Schuster and also worked with me on *Grant* and *Bush*. The manuscript was copyedited by Rick Willett.

I also owe a debt of gratitude to the "Gang of Thirteen"—old friends, former classmates, and colleagues who have read the manuscript and offered suggestions. Each brings a different perspective, and their suggestions have been invaluable: Richard Arndt, Robert Briskman '54, Jules Engel '54, Ellen Feldman, Beth Fischer, Peter Krogh, Sanford Lakoff, Peter Matson, Harry Moul '54, George Packard '54, Donald Rumsfeld '54, and David and Kelly Vaziri.

My agent once again was Peter Matson at Sterling Lord Literistic. Peter stands at the top of his profession and it is easy to see why. I am deeply indebted.

I have dedicated this book to my wife, Christine, whom I married in Berlin on September 24, 1959. I was stationed there with the army (I was a lieutenant in the field artillery), and Christine and I met at a party at the officers' club on New Year's Eve 1958. She was a student at the Free University, and we became engaged the following summer. In a sense, she is a war bride. But that is inadequate to describe the affection we have shared for sixty years.

Perhaps I should add that Christine's father, Johannes Zinsel, was captured in Paris at the Palais du Luxembourg. Mr. Zinsel was not a member of the SS, but was a high school teacher in Berlin who had been drafted into the German army in 1943 at the age of forty. He was assigned to a bookkeeping unit in Frankfurt, but in mid-August 1944 received orders to go to Paris and join another bookkeeping unit. When he got off the train in Paris on August 23 he was given a rifle and told to go to the Palais du Luxembourg. He was captured on August 25 and sent to an American prison camp in Normandy where, because he could speak English, he became a translator. He was eventually released from captivity in December 1945.

Notes

CHAPTER ONE—PARIS OCCUPIED

The epigraph is a statement Hitler made as he contemplated Paris from the Eglise du Sacré-Cœur on the morning of June 28, 1940. Arno Breker, *Paris, Hitler et moi* (Paris: Presses de la Cité, 1970), 97.

1 United States National Archives and Record Services, X *Nuremberg War Crimes Trials* (Washington, DC: General Services Administration, 1976), 519.

2 L'Institut Maurice-Thorez, *Des victoires de Hitler au triomphe de la démocratie et du socialisme; origines et bilan de la Deuxième Guerre mondiale* (Paris: Editions Sociales, 1970), 44.

3 Quoted in Jean-Pierre Azéma, *From Munich to the Liberation, 1938–1944* (London: Cambridge University Press, 1984), 32.

4 Article VIII, Armistice Agreement, June 22, 1940, U.S. Department of State, *Documents on German Foreign Policy, 1918–1945* (Washington, DC: Government Printing Office, 1956), 671–676.

5 William L. Shirer, *The Collapse of the Third Republic* (New York: Simon & Schuster, 1969), 1728.

6 Ibid., 900.

7 Robert O. Paxton, *Vichy France: Old Guard and New Order, 1940–1944* (New York: Alfred A. Knopf, 1972), 30.

8 H. R. Trevor-Roper, *Hitler's Table Talk, 1941–1944: His Private Conversations*, Norman Cameron and R. H. Stevens, trans. (New York: Enigma Books, 2000), 98–99.

9 Pierre Bourget, *Histoires secretes de l'Occupation de Paris, 1940–1944* (Paris: Hachette, 1970), 81–82.

10 Ronald C. Rosbottom, *When Paris Went Dark* (New York: Back Bay Books, 2014), 71.

11 Julian Jackson, *France: The Dark Years, 1940–1944* (New York: Oxford University Press, 2001), 171.

12 Alan Riding, *And the Show Went On: Cultural Life in Nazi-Occupied Paris* (New York: Random House, 2010), 57–63.

13 Azéma, *From Munich to the Liberation*, 58–59.

14 Shirer, *The Collapse of the Third Republic*, 761–762.

15 Charles de Gaulle, *The Call to Honour* (New York: Simon & Schuster, 1955), 83–84.

16 Jean Thouvenin, *Avec Pétain* (Paris: Sequana, 1940), 30, 33.

17 Riding, *And the Show Went On*, 93.

18 Albert Speer, *Au Coeur du Troisieme Reich* (Paris: Fayard, 1974), 371.

19 Azéma, *From Munich to the Liberation*, 121.

20 Rosbottom, *When Paris Went Dark*, 249.

21 Jacques Semelin, *Persécutions et Entraides dans la France Occupée* (Paris: Arènes-Senil, 2013), 245.

22 Jean-Paul Sartre, *Situations II* (Paris: Gallimard, 1948), 48–53.

23 Riding, *And the Show Went On*, 161–162.

24 Ibid.

25 Jackson, *France: The Dark Years*, 335.

26 Yves Bouthillier, *Le drame de Vichy II* (Paris: Plon, 1950), 7.

CHAPTER TWO—DE GAULLE AND THE RESISTANCE

The epigraph is a statement de Gaulle made to Eisenhower in their final meeting before Ike left North Africa for London and command of the invasion, December 30, 1943. Charles de Gaulle, *Unity* (New York: Simon & Schuster, 1959), 545.

1 Charles de Gaulle, *The Call to Honour* (New York: Viking, 1955), 75–77.

2 Francois Kersaudy, *Churchill and De Gaulle* (New York: Atheneum, 1982), 71.

3 De Gaulle, *The Call to Honour*, 72.

4 Antony Beevor and Artemis Cooper, *Paris After the Liberation, 1944–1949* (New York: Penguin, 2004), 5–6.

5 De Gaulle, *The Call to Honour*, 78.

6 Philippe de Gaulle, *De Gaulle: Mon Père* (Paris: Plon, 2008), 114–115.

7 De Gaulle, *The Call to Honour*, 82–83.

8 Ibid., 83–84.

9 Jean Lacouture, *De Gaulle: The Rebel, 1890–1944* (New York: Norton, 1990).

10 Kersaudy, *Churchill and De Gaulle*, 83.

11 *Cabinet Papers*, CAB 65/8, Supreme War Council, June 28, 1940.

12 Kersaudy, *Churchill and De Gaulle*, 90–91.

13 De Gaulle, *Call to Honour*, 128.

14 Ibid., 129.

15 Raoul Aglion, *Roosevelt and de Gaulle: Allies in Conflict, a Personal Memoir* (New York: Free Press, 1988), 115.

16 Ibid., 35, 184–190. Also see Charles L. Robertson, *When Roosevelt Planned to Govern France* (Amherst and Boston: University of Massachusetts Press, 2011); Milton Viorst, *Hostile Allies: FDR and Charles de Gaulle* (New York: Macmillan, 1965).

17 Kersaudy, *Churchill and De Gaulle*, 133.

18 *Chicago Daily News*, August 27, 1941.

19 *Prime Minister's Papers*, P.M. to Secretary of State, August 27, 1941.

20 British Foreign Office, Eden to Churchill, Note on C. de Gaulle, September 1, 1941.

21 Kersaudy, *Churchill and De Gaulle*, 160.

22 Cordell Hull, *The Memoirs of Cordell Hull II* (New York: Macmillan, 1948), 1130.

23 J. P. Lash, *Roosevelt and Churchill* (New York: Norton, 1976), 15–16.

24 De Gaulle, *Call to Honour*, 226.

25 Ibid., 230.

26 Ibid., 297.

27 Kersaudy, *Churchill and De Gaulle*, 187.

28 Julian Jackson, *France: The Dark Years, 1940–1944* (New York: Oxford University Press, 2001), 395.

29 De Gaulle, *Call to Honour*, 259.

30 William L. Langer, *Our Vichy Gamble* (New York: Knopf, 1947), 276–285, 305–335.

31 Jonathan Fenby, *France: A Modern History from the Revolution to the War with Terror* (New York: St. Martin's Press, 2015), 302.

32 Charles de Gaulle, *Unity* (New York: Simon & Schuster, 1959), 349–350.

33 Winston Churchill, *The Hinge of Fate* (Boston: Houghton Mifflin, 1952), 568.

34 Beevor and Cooper, *Paris After the Liberation*, 22–23.

35 *The Public Papers and Addresses of Franklin D. Roosevelt, Vol. XII: The Tide Turns 1943*, Samuel Rosenman, ed. (New York: Harper & Row, 1950), 83.

36 De Gaulle, *Unity*, 398.

37 Ibid., 399.

38 Churchill to Attlee and Eden, May 21, 1943, in Kersaudy, *Churchill and De Gaulle*, 279.

39 Anthony Eden, *The Reckoning* (London: Cassel, 1965), 386.

40 De Gaulle, *Unity*, 417.

41 Ibid., 424–425.

42 Warren F. Kimball, ed. *Churchill and Roosevelt: The Complete Correspondence* II (Princeton: Princeton University Press, 1984), 255.

43 FDR to Eisenhower, June 17, 1943, in Kersaudy, *Churchill and De Gaulle*, 289.

44 De Gaulle, *Unity*, 447.

45 Kersaudy, *Churchill and Roosevelt*, 297.

46 Ibid., 312.

47 De Gaulle, *Unity*, 547.

48 Ibid.

49 Harry Butcher, *My Three Years with Eisenhower* (New York: Simon & Schuster, 1946), 473.

50 De Gaulle, *Unity*, 547.

CHAPTER THREE—THE ALLIES ADVANCE

The epigraph is a statement Eisenhower made to David Schoenbrun in Gettysburg, Pennsylvania, August 25, 1964. Eisenhower Presidential Library.

1 Charles de Gaulle, *Unity* (New York: Simon & Schuster, 1959), 349–350.

2 Cable, Eisenhower to Marshall, January 19, 1944, *The Papers of Dwight David Eisenhower: The War Years* III (Baltimore: The Johns Hopkins Press, 1970), 1667.

3 Ibid., Note 2, 1667–1668.

4 McCloy to Eisenhower, April 15, 1944, *The War Years* III, Note 5, 1786. For the full text, see Harry L. Cole and Albert K. Weinberg, *Civil Affairs: Soldiers Become Governors* (Washington, DC: Center of Military History, 2004), 667–668.

5 Eisenhower, Memorandum for Record, March 22, 1944, *The War Years* III, 1783–1784.

6 De Gaulle, *Unity*, 544.

7 Eisenhower to Combined Chiefs of Staff, May 11, 1944, *The War Years* III, 1857–1858.

8 Roosevelt to Eisenhower, May 13, 1944, *The War Years* III, note 1, 1867–1868.

9 Eisenhower's cable to Roosevelt was in a message he sent to General Marshall, May 16, 1944, *The War Years* III, 1866–1867.

10 Dwight D. Eisenhower, *Crusade in Europe* (Garden City, NY: Doubleday, 1948), 248.

11 Eisenhower to de Gaulle, May 23, 1944, *The War Years* III, 1886.

12 De Gaulle to Eisenhower, May 27, 1944, *The War Years* III, note 3, 1886.

13 Churchill to Roosevelt, May 26, 1944, Warren F. Kimball, ed., *Churchill and Roosevelt: The Complete Correspondence* III, 145.

14 Roosevelt to Churchill, *Foreign Relations of the United States* 1944 (France) III, 694.

15 Churchill to Roosevelt, June 7, 1944, Kimball, *Churchill and Roosevelt* III, 171–172.

16 De Gaulle, *Unity*, 558.

17 Ibid., 560.

18 Eisenhower to Combined Chiefs, June 4, 1944, *The War Years* III, 1906–1907.

19 F. S. V. Dennison, *History of the Second World War, Civil Affairs and Military Government: Central Organization and Planning* (London: Her Majesty's Stationery Office, 1966), 69. Italics in original.

20 De Gaulle, *Unity*, 564.

21 Charles de Gaulle, *Discourses et Messages* I (Paris: Plon, 1974), 444.

22 "President Favors Delay on Algiers: Says Too Little Area Is Free to Consider de Gaulle Appointees at Present," *New York Times*, June 24, 1944.

23 Anthony Eden, *The Reckoning* (London: Cassell, 1965), 531.

24 Chester Wilmot, *Struggle for Europe* (New York: Harper & Row, 1952), 394–395.

25 Montgomery to Bradley, August 4, 1944, ibid., 400.

26 Eisenhower to Marshall, August 11, 1944, *The War Years* IV, 2066–2067.

27 John Keegan, *Six Armies in Normandy* (New York: Viking Press, 1982), 300–301. Also see William Mortimer Moore, *Free France's Lion: The Life*

of Philippe Leclerc, De Gaulle's Greatest General (Philadelphia: Casemate, 2011).

28 Eisenhower, *Crusade in Europe*, 279.

29 Omar Bradley and Clay Blair, *A General's Life* (New York: Simon & Schuster, 1983), 304.

30 Jean Lacouture, *De Gaulle: The Rebel 1890–1944* (New York: W. W. Norton, 1990), 546.

31 Charles de Gaulle, *Lettres, Notes et Carnets* IV (Paris: Plon, 1980), 289.

32 Ibid., 291–292.

33 De Gaulle, *Unity*, 631.

34 Eisenhower to Combined Chiefs of Staff, August 15, 1944, IV, *The War Years* 2069–2070.

35 Eden, *The Reckoning*, 544.

36 Lacouture, *De Gaulle: The Rebel*, 503.

37 De Gaulle, *Unity*, 636.

38 Ibid.

39 Ibid., 637.

40 The most complete survey of the Laval incident is provided by Charles L. Robertson in *When Roosevelt Planned to Govern France* (Amherst: University of Massachusetts Press, 2011), 180–184. Mr. Robertson is skeptical of de Gaulle's claim, but presents the evidence fairly.

41 De Gaulle, *Unity*, 637.

42 Ibid.

43 De Gaulle to Eisenhower, August 21, 1944, Eisenhower Library.

CHAPTER FOUR—THE GERMAN DEFENSE

The epigraph is from an order Hitler transmitted to Field Marshal Model on August 23, 1944. The entire message is reproduced in Dietrich von Choltitz, *Brennt Paris? Adolph Hitler* (Frankfurt/Main: R.G. Fischer Verlag, 2014), 1. This is a reprint of a book von Choltitz originally published in 1949.

1 Larry Collins and Dominique Lapierre, *Is Paris Burning?* (New York: Simon & Schuster, 1965), 24.

2 Dietrich von Choltitz, *Soldat Unter Soldaten* (Konstance: Europa Verlag, 1951), 222.

3 Collins and Lapierre, *Is Paris Burning?*, 27.

4 von Choltitz, *Soldat Unter Soldaten*, 222.

5 Ibid., 222.

6 Ibid., 223.

7 Collins and Lapierre, *Is Paris Burning?*, 29.

8 Michael Neiberg, *The Blood of Free Men* (New York: Basic Books, 2012), 87.

9 von Choltitz, *Soldat Unter Soldaten*, 226.

10 Ibid.

11 Randall Hansen, *Disobeying Hitler: German Resistance After Valkyrie* (New York: Oxford University Press, 2014), 77.

12 Ibid.

13 Ibid., 78.

14 von Choltitz, *Brennt Paris? Adolph Hitler* (Frankfurt/Main: R. G. Fischer Verlag, 2014), 32.

15 Ibid., 32–33.

16 Ibid., 24.

17 Ibid., 28.

18 Collins and Lapierre, *Is Paris Burning?*, 63–64.

19 von Choltitz, *Soldat Unter Soldaten*, 235.

20 Collins and Lapierre, *Is Paris Burning?*, 69–70.

21 von Choltitz, *Brennt Paris? Adolph Hitler*, 36.

22 Ibid., 37–38.

23 Hansen, *Disobeying Hitler*, 85, 88.

24 von Choltitz, *Soldat Unter Soldaten*, 238.

25 Ibid., 245.

26 Raoul Nordling, *Sauver Paris: Mémoires du Consul de Suède*, Fabrice Virgili, ed. (Brussels: Editions Complexe, 2002), 155.

27 Ibid., 156.

28 Adrien Dansette, *Histoire de la libération de Paris* (Paris: Librairie Arthème Fayard, 1958), 131.

29 von Choltitz, *Brennt Paris? Adolph Hitler*, 45–46.

30 Nordling, *Sauver Paris*, 179.

31 Ibid.

32 Ibid.

33 Dankwood Graf von Arnim, *Als Brandenburg noch die Mark hiess* (Munich: Goldmann Verlag, 1995), 245.

34 "*Résumé des journees glorieuses d'insurrection à la préfecture de police*," reprinted in Hansen, *Disobeying Hitler*, 97.

35 Ibid., 98.

36 Collins and Lapierre, *Is Paris Burning?*, 222.

37 Ibid., 151–152.

38 Ibid., 157.

39 Ibid., 194.

CHAPTER FIVE—THE RESISTANCE RISES

The epigraph is a statement made by General Dietrich von Choltitz in *Brennt Paris? Adolph Hitler* (Frankfurt/Main: R. D. Fischer Verlag, 2014), 52.

 1 Michael Neiberg, *The Blood of Free Men* (New York: Basic Books, 2012), 46.

 2 Colonel Henri Rol-Tanguy and Roger Bourderon, *La Libération de Paris* (Paris: Hachette, 1994), 140.

 3 Neiberg, *The Blood of Free Men*, 48.

 4 Ibid., 92.

 5 Ibid., 104.

 6 Matthew Cobb, *Eleven Days in August: The Liberation of Paris in 1944* (London: Simon & Schuster, 2013), 38.

 7 Ibid., 34.

 8 Rol-Tanguy and Bourderon, *La Libération de Paris*, 162.

 9 Pierre Taittinger, *Et Paris ne fut pas détruit* (Paris: L'Elan, 1948), 118–126.

10 Neiberg, *The Blood of Free Men*, 46.

11 Randall Hansen, *Disobeying Hitler: German Resistance After Valkyrie* (New York: Oxford University Press, 2014), 82.

12 Raoul Nordling, *Sauver Paris: Mémoires du Consul de Suède* (Brussels: Éditions Complexe, 2002), 94–95.

13 Martin Blumenson, ed., *The Patton Papers* II (Boston: Houghton Mifflin, 1974), 521.

14 Adrien Dansette, *Histoire de la Libération de Paris* (Paris: Librairie Arthème Fayard, 1958), 178.

15 Larry Collins and Dominique Lapierre, *Is Paris Burning?* (New York: Simon & Schuster, 1965), 110.

16 Dansette, *Histoire de la Libération de Paris*, 195.

17 Nordling, *Sauver Paris*, 115.

18 Henri Michel, *La Liberation de Paris* (Brussels: Éditions Complexe, 1980), 59.

19 Philippe Ragueneau and Eddy Florentin, eds. *Paris Libéré: Ils Étaient Là!* (Paris: France-Empire, 1994), 125.

20 Hansen, *Disobeying Hitler*, 95.

21 Collins and Lapierre, *Is Paris Burning?*, 164.

22 Ibid., 165.

23 Gilles Perrault and Pierre Azéma, *Paris Under the Occupation* (Paris: Vendôme, 1987), 52.

24 Robert Monod, *Les Heures Décisives de la Libération de Paris* (Paris: Editions Gilbert, 1947), 43.

25 Harold C. Lyon, "Operations of T-Force," Unit History 02-12-1949, U.S. Army Heritage and Education Center, Carlisle, Pennsylvania.

26 Collins and Lapierre, *Is Paris Burning?*, 182–183.

27 Danette, *Historie de la Libération de Paris*, 312. Also see "Le Récit de Gallois" in Philippe Ragueneau and Eddy Florentin, *Paris Libéré*, 218–219.

28 Collins and Lapierre, *Is Paris Burning?*, 183.

29 Neiberg, *The Blood of Free Men*, 184.

CHAPTER SIX—EISENHOWER CHANGES PLANS

The epigraph is a statement Eisenhower made to Bradley after receiving a letter from de Gaulle stressing the importance of liberating Paris. Quoted in Antony Beevor, *D-Day: The Battle for Normandy* (London: Viking, 2008), 494.

1 Rosalind Massow, "Ike and Mamie Talk About 50 Years of Marriage," *Parade*, June 26, 1966.

2 Ernest Hemingway, "Living on $1000 a Year in Paris," *Dateline Toronto: The Complete Toronto Star Dispatches, 1924–1928*, William White, ed. (New York: Scribner's, 1985), 88.

3 Mamie Eisenhower interview with John Wickman, Eisenhower Library; Jean Edward Smith, *Eisenhower in War and Peace* (New York: Random House, 2012), 60–76; Stephen Ambrose, *Eisenhower* (New York: Simon & Schuster, 1983), 75.

4 SHAEF Planning Staff, Post-NEPTUNE, Courses of Action After Capture of Lodgment Area, Sec. II, Method of Conducting the Campaign, 30 May, SGS SHAEF File 381, Post-OVERLORD Ping.

5   David Eisenhower, *Eisenhower at War, 1943–1945* (New York: Random House, 1986), 416.

6   De Gaulle to Eisenhower, August 21, 1944, Eisenhower Library.

7   Eisenhower to Combined Chiefs of Staff, August 22, 1944, *The Papers of Dwight David Eisenhower: The War Years* IV (Baltimore: Johns Hopkins Press, 1970), 2087–2089.

8   Omar N. Bradley and Clay Blair, *A General's Life* (New York: Simon & Schuster, 1983), 308–309.

9   Larry Collins and Dominique Lapierre, *Is Paris Burning?* (New York: Simon & Schuster, 1965), 185–186.

10 Antony Beevor, *D-Day: The Battle for Normandy* (London: Viking, 2008), 494.

11 Michael Neiberg, *The Blood of Free Men: The Liberation of Paris, 1944* (New York: Basic Books, 2012), 188.

12 Eisenhower, *The War Years* IV, 2089.

13 Ibid.

14 Ibid., 191.

15 Collins and Lapierre, *Is Paris Burning?*, 198.

16 Ibid., 198–199.

17 Ibid., 197.

18 Ibid., 215.

CHAPTER SEVEN—LECLERC MOVES OUT

The epigraph is a statement General Leclerc made to his G-3 operations officer after returning to his headquarters from a meeting with General Bradley on August 22, 1944. Larry Collins and Dominique Lapierre, *Is Paris Burning?* (New York: Simon & Schuster, 1965), 261.

1   Letter, Leclerc to Patton, August 14, 1944, on XV Corps C/S Journal and File, Center of Military History, Washington, DC.

2   Martin Blumenson, ed., *The Patton Papers, 1940–1945* (Boston: Houghton Mifflin, 1974), 511.

3   Martin Blumenson, *Breakout and Pursuit* (Washington, DC: Government Printing Office, 1960), 600.

4   Adrien Dansette, *Histoire de la Libération de Paris* (Paris: Librairie Arthème Fayard, 1958), 313.

5   Gerow to Leclerc, August 22, 1944, ibid., 314.

6 Rick Atkinson, *The Guns at Last Light* (New York: Henry Holt, 2013), 171–172.

7 Larry Collins and Dominique Lapierre, *Is Paris Burning?* (New York: Simon & Schuster, 1965), 203.

8 Ibid., 206.

9 Nelson Douglas Lankford, ed. *OSS Against the Reich: The World War II Diaries of Colonel David K. E. Bruce* (Kent, OH: Kent State University Press, 1993), 167–168.

10 Charles de Gaulle, *Unity: 1942–1944* (New York: Simon & Schuster, 1959), 643.

11 Atkinson, *The Guns at Last Light*, 172.

12 De Gaulle, *Unity*, 644.

13 Matthew Cobb, *Eleven Days in August* (New York: Simon & Schuster, 2013), 246.

14 Lankford, *Diaries of David K. E. Bruce*, 168–169.

15 Randall Hansen, *Disobeying Hitler: German Resistance After Valkyrie* (New York: Oxford University Press, 2014), 110.

16 Blumenson, *Breakout and Pursuit*, 614.

17 Atkinson, *The Guns at Last Light*, 172.

18 Omar N. Bradley, *A Soldier's Story* (New York: Henry Holt, 1951), 392.

19 William Mortimer Moore, *Free France's Lion: The Life of Philippe Leclerc, de Gaulle's Greatest General* (Philadelphia: Casemate, 2011), 298.

20 Ibid.

21 Raymond Dronne, *La Libération de Paris* (Paris: Presses de la Cité, 1970), 280–281.

22 Collins and Lapierre, *Is Paris Burning?*, 265.

23 Ibid.

24 Moore, *Free France's Lion*, 300.

25 Yvonne Féron, *Deliverance de Paris*, 42–43 (Paris: Hachette, 1945).

26 Pierre Crénesse, *La Libération des Ondes* (Paris: Berger-Levrault, 1944), 29–30.

27 Ibid., 33–34.

28 Dronne, *La Libération de Paris*, 285.

29 Jean-Christophe Notin, *Leclerc* (Paris: Perin, 2005), 269.

CHAPTER EIGHT—A FIELD OF RUINS

The epigraph is from Hitler's message to General Dietrich von Choltitz, August 23, 1944, in von Choltitz, *Brennt Paris? Adolph Hitler* (Frankfurt/Main: R. G. Fischer Verlag, 2014), 3.

1 Dietrich von Choltitz, *Brennt Paris? Adolph Hitler* (Frankfurt/Main: R. G. Fischer Verlag, 2014), 3.

2 Ibid., 72.

3 Matthew Cobb, *Eleven Days in August* (London: Simon & Schuster, 2013), 233.

4 Dietrich von Choltitz, *Soldat Unter Soldaten* (Konstance: Europa Verlag, 1951), 256–257.

5 von Choltitz, *Brennt Paris? Adolph Hitler*, 74.

6 von Choltitz, *Soldat Unter Soldaten*, 262.

7 Ibid.

8 von Choltitz, *Brennt Paris? Adolph Hitler*, 56–57.

9 Randall Hansen, *Disobeying Hitler: German Resistance After Valkyrie* (New York: Oxford University Press, 2014), 103–105.

10 Ibid., 82–83.

11 Ibid., 84.

12 Willis Thornton, *The Liberation of Paris* (New York: Harcourt, Brace & World, 1962), 171–172.

13 Cobb, *Eleven Days in August*, 234.

14 Ferdinand Dupuy, *La Libération de Paris vue d'un commissariat de police* (Paris: Librairies-Imprimeries reunies, 1945), 33–34.

15 De Saint-Pierre (pseudonym for Odette Lainville), *Des ténèbres à l'aube: journal d'une Française, Paris, 10 août–10 septembre 1944* (Paris: Arthaud, 1945), 84.

16 *L'Humanité*, August 23, 1944.

17 Hansen, *Disobeying Hitler*, 106.

18 Larry Collins and Dominique Lapierre, *Is Paris Burning?* (New York: Simon & Schuster, 1965), 230–231.

19 Ibid., 232.

20 Adrien Dansette, *Histoire de la Libération de Paris* (Paris: Librairie Arthème Fayard, 1958), 260–261.

21 von Choltitz, *Brennt Paris? Adolph Hitler*, 45–46.

22 Ibid., 86.

23 Ibid., 88.

24 Ibid., 75.

25 Cobb, *Eleven Days in August,* 508–509.

26 Collins and Lapierre, *Is Paris Burning?,* 295–296.

27 Hansen, *Disobeying Hitler,* 112–113.

28 von Choltitz, *Brennt Paris? Adolph Hitler,* 86.

29 Collins and Lapierre, *Is Paris Burning?,* 268–269.

30 von Choltitz, *Brennt Paris? Adolph Hitler,* 88.

31 Collins and Lapierre, *Is Paris Burning?,* 272.

CHAPTER NINE—DAY OF LIBERATION

The epigraph is from a newspaper article written by Ernie Pyle, August 25, 1944. David Nichols, ed., *Ernie's War: The Best of Ernie Pyle's World War II Dispatches* (New York: Touchstone, 1986), 351–352.

1 Randall Hansen, *Disobeying Hitler: German Resistance After Valkyrie* (New York: Oxford University Press, 2014), 115.

2 Klaus-Jürgen Müller, "*Die Befreiung von Paris und die deutsche Führung an der Westfront,*" in Michael Salewski and Guntram Schulze-Wegener, *Kriegsjahr 1944* (Stuttgart: Franz Steiner, 1995), 55.

3 Michael Neiberg, *The Blood of Free Men: The Liberation of Paris, 1944* (New York: Basic Books, 2012), 223.

4 Ibid.

5 Larry Collins and Dominique Lapierre, *Is Paris Burning?* (New York: Simon & Schuster, 1965), 298.

6 Ibid., 300.

7 Ibid., 301.

8 Ibid., 304.

9 Ibid., 308.

10 Dietrich von Choltitz, *Brennt Paris? Adolph Hitler* (Frankfurt/Main: R. D. Fischer Verlag, 2014), 91.

11 Ibid., 91.

12 Ibid., 92.

13 Ibid., 92–93.

14 Ibid., 93.

15 Quoted in Robert Aron, *France Reborn: The History of the Liberation* (New York: Charles Scribner's Sons, 1964), 291.

16 von Choltitz, *Brennt Paris? Adolph Hitler*, 95.

17 Ibid., 96.

18 Collins and Lapierre, *Is Paris Burning?*, 330.

19 William Mortimer Moore, *Free France's Lion: The Life of Philippe Leclerc, De Gaulle's Greatest General* (Havertown, PA: Casemate, 2011), 320.

20 Rick Atkinson, *The Guns at Last Light* (New York: Henry Holt, 2013), 179; Nelson D. Lankford, ed. *OSS Against the Reich: The World War II Diaries of David K. E. Bruce* (Kent, OH: Kent State University Press, 1991), 174; Martin Blumenson, *Liberation* (Alexandria, VA: Time-Life, 1978), 156.

21 Charles de Gaulle, *Unity* (New York: Simon & Schuster, 1959), 646.

22 Ibid., 346–347.

23 Moore, *Free France's Lion*, 311.

24 De Gaulle, *Unity*, 647.

25 Moore, *Free France's Lion*, 311.

26 De Gaulle, *Unity*, 647–648.

27 Collins and Lapierre, *Is Paris Burning?*, 333.

28 De Gaulle, *Unity*, 649.

29 Ibid.

30 The text of de Gaulle's speech is in Neiberg, *The Blood of Free Men*, 237–238.

31 De Gaulle, *Unity*, 650.

32 Ibid.

33 Jean Lacouture, *De Gaulle: The Rebel, 1890–1944* (New York: W. W. Norton, 1990), 575.

34 Moore, *Free France's Lion*, 314.

35 Matthew Cobb, *Eleven Days in August* (London: Simon & Schuster, 2013), 312.

36 Matthew Cobb, *The Resistance: The French Fight Against the Nazis* (London: Pocket Books, 2009), 269.

37 David Nichols, ed., *Ernie's War: The Best of Ernie Pyle's World War II Dispatches* (New York: Touchstone, 1986), 353.

38 Albert Camus, *Actuelles Chroniques, 1944–1948* (Paris: Gallimard, 1950), 22.

CHAPTER TEN—DE GAULLE TRIUMPHANT

The epigraph is a statement by Eisenhower after meeting with de Gaulle in Paris on August 27, 1944. Larry Collins and Dominique Lapierre, *Is Paris Burning?* (New York: Simon & Schuster, 1965), 354.

1 *L'Humanite*, August 26, 1944.

2 Charles de Gaulle, *Unity* (New York: Simon & Schuster, 1964), 651–652.

3 Gerow to Leclerc, Orders, August 26, 1944, reprinted in Martin Blumenson, *Breakout and Pursuit* (Washington, DC: Government Printing Office, 1960), 620.

4 Adrien Dansette, *Histoire de la Libération de Paris* (Paris: Librairie Arthème Fayard, 1958), 403.

5 De Gaulle, *Unity*, 652.

6 Simone de Beauvoir, *La Force des choses* (Paris: Gallimard, 1963), 612.

7 De Gaulle, *Unity*, 654.

8 Pascale Moisson, *Anecdotes . . . sous la Botte* (Paris: L'Hamattan, 1998), 128.

9 De Gaulle, *Unity*, 657.

10 Graham Robb, *Parisians: An Adventure History of Paris* (New York: W. W. Norton, 2010), 319.

11 Larry Collins and Dominique Lapierre, *Is Paris Burning?* (New York: Simon & Schuster, 1965), 352.

12 William Mortimer Moore, *Free France's Lion* (Havertown, PA: Casemate, 2011), 318.

13 Collins and Lapierre, *Is Paris Burning?*, 352.

14 De Gaulle, *Unity*, 658.

15 Collins and Lapierre, *Is Paris Burning?*, 354.

16 De Gaulle to Eisenhower, August 26, 1944, Eisenhower Presidential Library.

17 Kay Summersby, *Eisenhower Was My Boss* (New York: Prentice-Hall, 1948), 175.

18 David Eisenhower, *Eisenhower at War, 1943–1945* (New York: Random House, 1986), 427.

19 Kay Summersby, *Past Forgetting: My Love Affair with Dwight D. Eisenhower* (New York: Simon & Schuster, 1975), 211.

20 Omar N. Bradley, *A Soldier's Story* (New York: Henry Holt, 1951), 394.

21 Summersby, *Past Forgetting*, 211.

22 Merle Miller, *Ike the Soldier* (New York: G.P. Putnam, 1987), 682.

23 Summersby, *Past Forgetting*, 212.

24 Miller, *Ike the Soldier*, 682.

25 Summersby, *Eisenhower Was My Boss*, 176.

26 Eisenhower interview with David Schoenbrun, August 25, 1964, Eisenhower Presidential Library.

27 Dwight D. Eisenhower, *Crusade in Europe* (New York: Doubleday, 1948), 298.

28 De Gaulle, *Unity*, 662.

29 Ibid.

30 Collins and Lapierre, *Is Paris Burning?*, 354.

31 Blumenson, *Breakout and Pursuit*, 625.

32 Eisenhower to Marshall, August 31, 1944, *The Papers of Dwight David Eisenhower: The War Years* IV (Baltimore: The Johns Hopkins Press, 1970), 2108.

33 Bradley, *A Soldier's Story*, 396.

34 Summersby, *Eisenhower Was My Boss*, 178.

35 De Gaulle, *Unity*, 660.

36 Montgomery to Field Marshal Sir Alan Brooke, August 18, 1944, in Nigel Hamilton, *Master of the Battlefield: Monty's War Years* (London: Hamish Hamilton, 1983), 798. Brooke, who held a position similar to George Marshall, replied the next day: "I completely agree." Ibid., 799.

37 John Russell Young, *Around the World with General Grant* I (New York: American News Company, 1879), 416–417.

Bibliography

Aglion, Raoul. *Roosevelt and de Gaulle: Allies in Conflict, A Personal Memoir.* New York: Free Press, 1988.

Ambrose, Stephen. *Eisenhower.* New York: Simon & Schuster, 1983.

Aron, Robert. *France Reborn: The History of the Liberation.* New York: Charles Scribner's Sons, 1964.

Article VIII, Armistice Agreement, June 22, 1940. U.S. Department of State, *Documents on German Foreign Policy, 1918–1945.* Washington, DC: Government Printing Office, 1956.

Atkinson, Rick. *The Guns at Last Light.* New York: Henry Holt, 2013.

Azéma, Jean-Pierre. *From Munich to the Liberation, 1938–1944.* London: Cambridge University Press, 1984.

Beevor, Antony, and Artemis Cooper. *Paris After the Liberation, 1944–1949.* New York: Penguin, 2004.

Blumenson, Martin. *Breakout and Pursuit.* Washington, DC: Government Printing Office, 1960.

———. *Liberation.* Alexandria, VA: Time-Life, 1978.

———. *The Patton Papers.* 2 vols. Boston: Houghton Mifflin, 1974.

Bourget, Pierre. *Histoires secretes de l'Occupation de Paris, 1940–1944.* Paris: Hachette, 1970.

Bouthillier, Yves. *La drame de Vichy.* Vol. 2. Paris: Plon, 1950.

Bradley, Omar N. *A Soldier's Story.* New York: Henry Holt, 1951.

Bradley, Omar N., and Clay Blair. *A General's Life.* New York: Simon & Schuster, 1983.

Breker, Arno. *Paris, Hitler et moi.* Paris: Presses de la Cité, 1970.

Butcher, Henry. *My Three Years with Eisenhower.* New York: Simon & Schuster, 1946.

Camus, Albert. *Actuelles Chroniques, 1944–1948.* Paris: Gallimard, 1950.

Churchill, Winston S. *The Hinge of Fate.* Boston: Houghton Mifflin, 1952.

————. *Their Finest Hour.* Boston: Houghton Mifflin, 1949.

Cobb, Matthew. *Eleven Days in August.* London: Simon & Schuster, 2013.

————. *The Resistance: The French Fight Against the Nazis.* London: Pocket Books, 2009.

Cole, Harry L., and Albert K. Weinberg. *Civil Affairs: Soldiers Become Governors.* Washington, DC: Center of Military History, 2004.

Collins, Larry, and Dominique Lapierre. *Is Paris Burning?* New York: Simon & Schuster, 1965.

Dansette, Adrien. *Histoire de la Libération de Paris.* Paris: Arthème Fayard, 1958.

De Beauvoir, Simone. *La Force des choses.* Paris: Gallimard, 1963.

De Gaulle, Charles. *The Call to Honour.* New York: Simon & Schuster, 1955.

————. *Lettres, Notes et Carnets.* Paris: Plon, 1980.

————. *Discourses et Messages.* Paris: Plon, 1974.

————. *Unity.* New York: Simon & Schuster, 1959.

De Gaulle, Philippe. *De Gaulle: Mon Père.* Paris: Plon, 2008.

De Saint-Pierre (pseudonym for Odette Lainville). *Des ténèbres à l'aube: journal d'une Française, Paris, 10 août–10 septembre 1944.* Paris: Arthaud, 1945.

Dennison, F. S. V. *History of the Second World War, Civil Affairs and Military Government: Central Organization and Planning.* London: Her Majesty's Stationery Office, 1966.

Dronne, Raymond. *La Libération de Paris.* Paris: Presses de la Cité, 1970.

Dupuy, Ferdinand. *La Libération de Paris vue d'un commissariat de police.* Paris: Librairies-Imprimeries reunies, 1945.

Eden, Anthony. *The Reckoning.* London: Cassel, 1965.

Eisenhower, David. *Eisenhower at War, 1943–1945.* New York: Random House, 1986.

Eisenhower, Dwight David. *Crusade in Europe.* New York: Doubleday, 1948.

————. *The Papers of Dwight David Eisenhower: The War Years.* Baltimore: Johns Hopkins Press, 1970.

Fenby, Jonathan. *France: A Modern History from the Revolution to the War with Terror.* New York: St. Martin's Press, 2015.

Hamilton, Nigel. *Master of the Battlefield: Monty's War Years.* London: Hamish Hamilton, 1983.

Hansen, Randall. *Disobeying Hitler: German Resistance After Valkyrie.* New York: Oxford University Press, 2014.

Hatch, Alden. *Red Carpet for Mamie.* New York: Henry Holt, 1954.

Hull, Cordell. *Memoirs of Cordell Hull.* 2 vols. New York: Macmillan, 1948.

Jackson, Julian. *France: The Dark Years, 1940–1944.* New York: Oxford University Press, 2001.

———. *De Gaulle.* Cambridge: Harvard University Press, 2018.

Kersaudy, Francois. *Churchill and De Gaulle.* New York: Atheneum, 1982.

Kimball, Warren F., ed. *Churchill and Roosevelt: The Complete Correspondence.* 2 vols. Princeton: Princeton University Press, 1984.

Lacouture, Jean. *De Gaulle: The Rebel, 1890–1944.* New York: W.W. Norton, 1990.

Lankford, Nelson Douglas. *OSS Against the Reich: The World War II Diaries of Colonel David K. E. Bruce.* Kent, OH: Kent State University Press, 1993.

Lash, J. P. *Roosevelt and Churchill.* New York: Norton, 1976.

L'Institut Maurice-Thorez. *Des victoires de Hitler au triomphe de la démocratie et du socialisme; origines et bilan de la Deuxième Guerre mondiale.* Paris: Editions Sociales, 1970.

Lyon, Harold C. "Operations of T-Force," Unit History 02-12-1949. U.S. Army Heritage and Education Center, Carlisle, Pennsylvania.

Michel, Henri. *La Libération de Paris.* Brussels: Éditions Complexe, 1980.

Miller, Merle. *Ike the Soldier.* New York: G.P. Putnam, 1987.

Moisson, Pascale. *Anecdotes . . . sous la Botte.* Paris: L'Hamattan, 1998.

Monod, Robert. *Les Heures Décisives de la Libération de Paris.* Paris: Editions Gilbert, 1947.

Moore, William Mortimer. *Free France's Lion: The Life of Philippe Leclerc, de Gaulle's Greatest General.* Philadelphia: Casemate, 2011.

Neiberg, Michael. *The Blood of Free Men.* New York: Basic Books, 2012.

Nichols, David, ed. *Ernie's War: The Best of Ernie Pyle's World War II Dispatches.* New York: Touchstone, 1986.

Nordling, Raoul. *Sauver Paris: Mémoires du consul de Suède.* Fabrice Virgili, ed. Brussels: Editions Complexe, 2002.

Paxton, Robert O. *Vichy France: Old Guard and New Order, 1940–1944.* New York: Alfred A. Knopf, 1972.

Perrault, Gilles, and Pierre Azéma. *Paris Under the Occupation.* Paris: Vendôme, 1987.

Ragueneau, Philippe, and Eddy Florentin, eds. *Paris Libéré: Ils Étaient Là!* Paris: France-Empire, 1994.

Riding, Alan. *And the Show Went On: Cultural Life in Nazi-Occupied Paris.* New York: Random House, 2010.

Robb, Graham. *Parisians: An Adventure History of Paris.* New York: W. W. Norton, 2010.

Robertson, Charles L. *When Roosevelt Planned to Govern France.* Amherst: University of Massachusetts Press, 2011.

Rol-Tanguy, Colonel Henri, and Roger Bourderon. *La Libération de Paris.* Paris: Hachette, 1994.

Rosbottom, Ronald C. *When Paris Went Dark.* New York: Back Bay Books, 2014.

Rosenman, Samuel, ed. *The Public Papers and Addresses of Franklin D. Roosevelt, 1943: The Tide Turns.* New York: Harper & Row, 1950.

Salewski, Michael, and Guntram Schulze-Wegener. *Kriegsjahr 1944.* Stuttgart: Franz Steiner, 1995.

Sartre, Jean-Paul. *Situations II.* Paris: Gallimard, 1948.

Semelin, Jacques. *Persécutions et Entraides dans la France Occupée.* Paris: Arènes-Senil, 2013.

Shirer, William L. *The Collapse of the Third Republic.* New York: Simon & Schuster, 1969.

Smith, Jean Edward. *Eisenhower in War and Peace.* New York: Random House, 2012.

———. *Lucius D. Clay: An American Life.* New York: Henry Holt, 1990.

Speer, Albert. *Au Coeur du Troisième Reich.* Paris: Fayard, 1974.

Speidel, Hans. *We Defended Normandy.* London: Herbert Jenkins, 1951.

Summersby, Kay. *Eisenhower Was My Boss.* New York: Prentice-Hall, 1948.

———. *Past Forgetting: My Love Affair with Dwight D. Eisenhower.* New York: Simon & Schuster, 1975.

Taittinger, Pierre. *Et Paris ne fut pas détruit.* Paris: L'Elan, 1948.

Thouvenin, Jean. *Avec Pétain.* Paris: Sequana, 1940.

Trevor-Roper, H. R. *Hitler's Table Talk, 1941–1944: His Private Conversations.* Norman Cameron and R. H. Stevens, trans. New York: Enigma Books, 2000.

United States National Archives and Record Services X. *Nuremberg War Crimes Trials.* Washington, DC: General Services Administration, 1976.

Von Arnim, Dankwood Graf. *Als Brandenburg noch die Mark hiess.* Munich: Goldmann Verlag, 1995.

Von Choltitz, Dietrich. *Brennt Paris? Adolph Hitler.* Frankfurt/Main: R. G. Fischer Verlag, 2014. This is a reprint of a book originally published by von Choltitz in 1949.

————. *Soldat Unter Soldaten.* Konstanz: Europa Verlag, 1951.

Westphal, Siegfried. *The German Army in the West.* London: Cassell, 1951.

Wilmot, Chester. *Struggle for Europe.* New York: Harper & Row, 1952.

Young, John Russell. *Around the World with General Grant.* Vol. 1. New York: American News Company, 1879.

Index

Page numbers in *italics* refer to photographs and illustrations.

Photo Credits

"That rarest and most welcome of historians, one who addresses a serious popular readership without sacrificing high scholarly standards."

—THE WASHINGTON POST

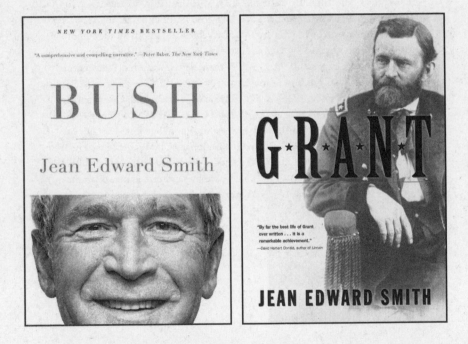

Available wherever books are sold
or at SimonandSchuster.com

SIMON &
SCHUSTER